Other Works by Michael Aaron Rockland

Nonfiction

Sarmiento's Travels in the United States in 1847 (1970)

America in the Fifties and Sixties: Julian Marias on the United States (editor) (1972)

The American Jewish Experience in Literature (1975)

Homes on Wheels (1980)

Looking for America on the New Jersey Turnpike (co-authored with Angus Kress Gillespie) (1989)

Snowshoeing Through Sewers (1994)

What's American About American Things? (1996)

Popular Culture: Or Why Study "Trash"? (1999)

The Jews of New Jersey: A Pictorial History (co-authored with Patricia M. Ard) (2001)

Fiction

A Bliss Case (1989)

Screenplay

Three Days on Big City Waters (co-authored with Charles Woolfolk) (1974)

The George Washington Bridge

Poetry in Steel

Michael Aaron Rockland

RIVERGATE BOOKS
An imprint of Rutgers University Press
New Brunswick, New Jersey, and London

Library of Congress Cataloging-in-Publication Data

Rockland, Michael Aaron.
The George Washington Bridge : poetry in steel / Michael Aaron Rockland.
    p.   cm.
Includes bibliographical references and index.
ISBN 978–0–8135–4375–8 (hardcover : alk. paper)
   1. George Washington Bridge (New York, N.Y.) 2. Bridges—New York (State)—
  New York—Design and construction—History. I. Title.
TG25.N515R63 2008
624.2'3097471—dc22

2008000897

A British Cataloging-in-Publication record for this book is available from the British
Library.

Title page photograph courtesy of the Port Authority.

Visit our Web site: http://rutgerspress.rutgers.edu

Manufactured in the United States of America
Design and composition: Jack Donner, BookType

For Alana, Jessica, Jacob, Talia, Shira, Maliwan, and Jangila
The Future Is Now

"The George Washington . . .
is the most beautiful bridge in the world"
—Le Corbusier

Contents

The George Washington Bridge

The world from on high in one of the towers. Courtesy of the Port Authority.

Introduction

I HAVE LIVED MOST OF MY LIFE ON ONE SIDE OR THE OTHER of the George Washington Bridge. It is the busiest bridge in the world and, since its 1931 inauguration, has gotten steadily busier. Some 108 million vehicles crossed it in 2007, utilizing its two decks and fourteen lanes. Many people have deep affection for it and consider it the most beautiful bridge in the world. The George Washington, which celebrated its seventy-fifth anniversary in 2006, is in a class of its own.

When I was a young boy growing up in the Bronx, I knew about the bridge because vegetable-laden horse-drawn wagons, having crossed it from New Jersey, regularly wandered through my Bronx neighborhood. Cries were directed up to the windows of each apartment building: "New Jersey fresh; New Jersey fresh." My mother would lean out the window and tell the farmers what she wanted and then, grabbing her pocketbook, go downstairs to complete the purchases. Egg vendors also came across the bridge from New Jersey and went door-to-door in our building. My mother bought from them too. "Direct from the hen," she would say. In those days it seemed perfectly valid for New Jersey to call itself "the Garden State." And for New Yorkers, the pathway to that garden's bounty was the George Washington Bridge.

My father would often talk about being at the George Washington as a pedestrian when it opened for traffic on October 25, 1931. That day 57,788 vehicles and one man on a horse crossed the bridge. Tolls for automobiles and horse-and-wagons were an identical fifty cents, but the policemen who were then the toll collectors were unsure whether to

3

charge the man on horseback fifty or the twenty-five charged for bicy-cles. After some discussion, they elected the latter. Ten cents was charged for pedestrians on the walkways, though the shuttle bus ride across the bridge was only a nickel.

Years later my father was still commenting on this irony. "It cost more to walk across it than to ride the bus across it," he would say indignantly. He always planned to write the Port Authority to complain. Perhaps he did, because eventually the pedestrian toll dropped to a nickel and later

Photo of the author (on right) at age five on the George Washington Bridge, his older brother on the left.

was abandoned altogether, while the fare for the bus went up steadily and today is a dollar. My father, as if he had a proprietary interest in it, followed all news of the George. For him, it was *the* bridge.

As it was for my boyhood friends and me. We often took a trolley to the Bronx's limits on the Harlem River and trekked across this skinny portion of Manhattan, which here, between the Harlem and Hudson rivers, is only a mile and a quarter wide. We would access one of the two bridge walkways that flank the Upper Level and begin hiking to New Jersey. We could see the great buildings of Manhattan stretching to the south and the dark Palisades of New Jersey directly to the west. The sparkling Hudson rushed by beneath us, with far more river traffic than you see today—tugs and freighters and oil barges and pleasure boats—but our eyes were especially drawn, directly in front of us, to the lattice-like steel girders of the giant bridge towers.

The towers reminded us of our Erector Set projects. Indeed, from the moment the George Washington Bridge was inaugurated in 1931 the picture on Erector Set boxes was of a father and son working together on a miniature G.W.B. tower with a painting of the bridge itself in the background. The message was clear: when they grew up, those with Erector Sets would do great things. Dr. Margot Ammann Durrer, daughter of Othmar Ammann, remembers her father, years after he had designed and built the George Washington Bridge, "constructing a model of a G.W.B. tower with my brothers using their Erector Set."[1] My own father and I—like Ammann and his sons and the father and son on the box—tried to make a George Washington Bridge tower with the Erector Set he had bought me for my birthday. Eventually, we gave up because the project was so complicated. No other bridge has such complex and interesting towers. As we shall see in chapter 5, "The Accidental Icon," there is quite a story behind why the towers look as they do.

Hiking toward the towers, my friends and I were alternately thrilled and frightened as our walkway bounced up and down in response to traffic and weather. The bridge's roadways can oscillate by as much as three feet. The giant barrel cables from which they hang, two on the north side and two on the south, bow slightly under the weight. Motorists on the bridge, especially on warm summer days when steel expands, nervously notice this effect whenever congestion brings traffic to a halt. Is something the matter with their car? Why is it bouncing so jerkily? What if they break down on the George

Washington Bridge? Few realize that the bridge itself is making their car act strangely. But no matter: once they're off the bridge and those strange movements cease, a trip to the mechanic is put off and eventually forgotten.

The bridge for my friends and me didn't just move, it made sounds. The wind buffeting the towers and cables caused them to emit strange noises. David Shayt, of the National Museum of American History, says the sounds remind him of those produced by a tuning fork, but the image my friends and I entertained was of a giant harp.[2] That "harp," like any suspension bridge, seemed like a goofy Rube Goldberg concoction designed to defy gravity. Wasn't there a simpler way to build a bridge, we wondered, than to erect towers that touch the sky, run what appear to be giant clotheslines over them, and then hang roadways off the lines?

After my friends and I crossed the George to the New Jersey side, we would camp out in the woods on the crest of the Palisades in the Fort Lee area, not yet covered with high-rise apartment buildings. Few people today think about a fort when they say "Fort Lee," but what is now a small city was an important fort during the American Revolution. Fort Lee was named for General Charles Lee, second in command of the American army. Thomas Paine, then an aide to General Nathanael Greene, who commanded the 2,667 troops stationed there, wrote the inflammatory pamphlet *The American Crisis* at the fort, with its crucial line "These are the times that try men's souls" and its famous references to "summer soldiers" and "sunshine patriots."

A disconsolate George Washington stood in Fort Lee in November 1776 watching the British surround and capture Fort Washington on the New York side of the Hudson in the area of Manhattan we now call Washington Heights. While he held both forts, Washington could control access to the Hudson River with cannon. But with the bulk of his bedraggled army he had been forced to escape across the Hudson to Fort Lee at almost exactly the spot where the bridge that bears his name now stands. Soon he would also abandon Fort Lee and retreat across New Jersey and into Pennsylvania, the British in hot pursuit.

The Revolutionary War was at a desperate stage at this point, with one American defeat after another. Hungry for some kind of victory, however humble, Washington, by late December, would recross the Delaware, cleverly circumvent the main British army, and defeat the Hessians at Trenton, following this by defeating another minor force of enemy troops occupying Princeton. He would be back in Fort Lee in 1781, preparing to cross the Hudson again to engage the British in Manhattan.

Thus the George Washington Bridge stretches from one Revolutionary War fort site to another. The New York tower stands in Fort Washington Park, the New Jersey tower just offshore from where Fort Lee once stood on the Palisades. At the G.W.B.'s inauguration on October 24, 1931, New York governor Franklin Roosevelt—soon to be president of the United States—said, "We may rejoice that this bridge is at a site so sacred to patriotic memories."[3]

But for my friends and me, city boys, crossing the bridge to Fort Lee was simply going to "the country." In the woods of Palisades Interstate Park, accessible from the north walkway, we would make a fire and cook skewers of meat and apples and onions. As evening came on and the sun sank behind us, we observed the color of the bridge changing from silver to purple to orange. When we awoke in our pup tents in the morning, there the bridge still was, the sun, as it rose in the east, placing the towers in silhouette while the great city across the Hudson came alive. Though we were too young to express it in this manner, we marveled at the scene the bridge presented of the built environment and nature combining so harmoniously.

Most of my adult life has been spent on the New Jersey side of the bridge. The bridge has been, in a sense, an indispensable link between my two selves—as much metaphor as means of crossing the Hudson. I have traversed it numerous times on foot and by bicycle and perhaps a thousand times by automobile.

Often I have elected the bridge even when it would have been more convenient to take the Holland or Lincoln Tunnel en route to midtown or Lower Manhattan to see a play, attend a concert, or check out an art exhibit. Bridges, especially the George Washington, make me happy. They express in physical form one of the noblest impulses of mankind—to reach across barriers. I approach a bridge with anticipated pleasure. George Bailey, played by Jimmy Stewart in the movie *It's a Wonderful Life*, was speaking to me when he reasserted his belief in life by saying, "I'm going to build things.... I'm going to build bridges a mile long."[4]

While recognizing tunnels as a technological achievement, I don't feel the same way about them. In tunnels I'm anxious to get to the other end—only beginning to relax when I see a distant light beckoning—whereas on a bridge I drive as slowly as I dare to prolong the experience.

Bridges soar; tunnels burrow. As John Teel, a retired electrician who spent most of his working years on the G.W.B., once said to me, "A bridge is like an airplane. A tunnel is a hole in the ground."[5]

The George Washington was also for many years my path to twice-monthly visits to my aged mother, still living in the old Bronx neighborhood. From my mother's balcony, looking west, I could see the gleaming towers of the bridge I had driven across shortly before. They were as tall as sixty-story skyscrapers and even more imposing, standing astride the Hudson River on their great legs. From that perspective the towers were not only spectacular; they had an ominous quality. They reminded me of the Martian war machines in H. G. Wells's *War of the Worlds*, which in Orson Welles's 1938 radio version marched across New Jersey. It was as if the towers had done just that and now were hesitating, one having forded the great river, the other as yet uncertain whether to proceed.

It was usually dark on my return trip to New Jersey, and I would anticipate with pleasure the double necklace of 148 emerald-green mercury-vapor lights that decorates the two outside barrel cables. The lights were extinguished during World War II because they made the bridge a perfect target for aerial attack. Destroying the G.W.B. then, as now, would have crippled the metropolitan area because it was and remains the only bridge directly connecting New Jersey and the continent beyond to Manhattan Island. I would also look forward to seeing the bright Will Rogers–Wiley Post beacon whose beam extends out sixty-four miles from atop the New York tower and has guided planes into Greater New York's airports since 1935.[6]

Before 2000 the towers themselves were illuminated from below by searchlights, but in celebration of the millennium, they were ingeniously lit from within, each with 380 1,000-watt lights, some say in imitation of the Eiffel Tower in Paris but, for me, more beautiful given their dramatic setting. Those crystalline lights were turned on for the first time at sunset on July 4, 2000. Now, on national holidays, they glow brightly from the towers, making them appear to be encrusted with diamonds. The bridge is beautiful by day; by night the George is magical.

In New Jersey and New York, we're all on a first-name basis with "the George," a.k.a. "the G.W. Bridge," "the G.W.B.," "the G.W.," and "the Geo." For some of us—especially people in the Bronx, Upper Manhattan, and New Jersey, not to mention truckers and other motorists embarking on or terminating a transcontinental trip—it's simply "the bridge," like New York is "the city." The famed Brooklyn Bridge is hardly on our radar screens.

Nevertheless, when I visited my public library a few years ago seeking a book on the George Washington, I found none. I wanted to read up on the bridge, to find out more about who built it, how it worked—not just to enjoy it but to understand it, nuts and bolts. The library had a whole section of books on bridges, some going back to the very earliest—those nature created when trees fell across rivers, others that native peoples spun with fibers across gorges in the Andes, two-thousand-year-old Roman bridges that still stand. I counted no fewer than five books on the Brooklyn Bridge, one on the Triborough Bridge, and another on the Verrazano, just to mention bridges around New York City. Many of the general books by bridge aficionados contained chapters on the George Washington, but there was no book on the George itself. I checked my county library with the same results. I checked the library of the university where I teach; I went online. Again, no luck. I couldn't quite believe it. I had always thought the George to be as important, not just from an engineering perspective but culturally and historically and aesthetically as well, as any bridge in the world.[7] I decided that if I really wanted to know about the George Washington Bridge I would have to research and write the book myself.

But writing a book about it in today's world is easier said than done. The 1993 bombers of the World Trade Center had the George Washington Bridge on their list for future terrorist attacks. And when 9/11 happened eight years later, the Port Authority of New York and New Jersey tragically lost eighty-four of its personnel, some of whom would have had much to tell me about the bridge. The Authority also lost the greater part of its eighty years (1921–2001) of archives and old photographs when the Twin Towers, where it was headquartered, and which it financed and managed, were destroyed.

Security issues in our post-9/11 world played an important role in the writing of this book. Even though earlier in my career I had a top secret clearance from the federal government, it took four months before I was vetted by the Port Authority, and even then I was aware that on the bridge I was under surveillance. Someone hanging out on the bridge walkways is, understandably, regarded suspiciously; there are signs everywhere that say NO LOITERING. I have in recent years, while studying the bridge, definitely "loitered" on it, though I have been scrupulous in obeying the signs that say CAMERA USE PROHIBITED— except once, but we'll get to that later. Martin Bruch, a handicapped Austrian, found out the hard way that picture taking on the G.W.B. is just not done these days. His film, *Handbike Movie,* details his travels around the world on a hand-propelled adult tricycle with a camera mounted on his helmet. When he gets to the George Washington and attempts to ride across on the walkway, an officer stops him and forbids him to photograph anything.[8]

More than once it has occurred to me while on the bridge that security personnel who might not know of my clearance were wondering why I was studying the bridge so intently. If not a terrorist, was I contemplating suicide? The G.W.B. averages slightly more than one "successful" suicide per month and several attempts foiled by bridge authorities taking quick action.

Eighty-six Port Authority policemen are now assigned to the bridge. They are supported by hundreds of closed circuit television cameras on the bridge and on the nearest high-rise buildings in Fort Lee and Manhattan. In the lobby of the bridge offices overlooking the bridge in Fort Lee is the Communications Center where the bridge is monitored 24/7 with the most sophisticated technology available. If you were to pick up any of the sixty-nine emergency phones on the bridge, a camera would immediately zoom in on you to size up the situation you might be reporting.

Security is paramount, and it is tight. Ken Philmus, once general manager of the G.W.B. and, on 9/11, director of the Port Authority's Division of Tunnels, Bridges, and Terminals, found his job considerably different after the tragedy. "I'm a transportation guy," he said. "Now I had to devote much of my time and our resources to security. And security is one big toilet bowl; you get nothing positive out of it."[9] The Authority spends half a billion dollars more per year on security for its bi-state facilities—its bridges and tunnels and airports and trains and the port itself—than it was spending before 9/11. We'd do well to remember that when we complain about increased tolls and fees.

Despite heightened security, I was granted two opportunities to experience the most sensitive and interesting places on and around the bridge. It is one thing as a writer to gather the facts about a subject, quite another to clamber about on it—to know it quite literally top to bottom rather than just reading everything available and interviewing knowledgeable people about it. Thus this book combines scholarship on the one hand and adventure on the other. Something of the personal intrudes in virtually every chapter—in part because of my affection for the bridge and a lifetime of experiencing it but also because of the days on the bridge to which authorities treated me. The first of these follows as chapter 1.

MICHAEL AARON ROCKLAND

Morristown, New Jersey
February 2008

The bridge in fog in 1962, the Lower Level now in place. Courtesy of the Port Authority.

A Day on the G.W.B.

ON APRIL 11, 2006, Robert Durando, general manager of the George Washington Bridge, and Robert McKee, physical plant manager, took me on a tour of bridge facilities the public never sees, some of which I didn't know existed. As general manager, Durando supervises some 220 full-time staff members (not including the 86 bridge police) while McKee, one of two key assistants to Durando (the other is concerned with daily operations such as toll collecting), manages regular and long-range maintenance.

It was Opening Day at Yankee Stadium, and Durando and McKee had agreed to accompany me in the hours after New Jersey fans had already passed over the bridge and before they would be coming back from the Bronx. We could hear fighter jets tearing through the sky over the Bronx, part of the Opening Day festivities. When the Yankees are playing a home game, the bridge staff is on alert. McKee told me, "We coordinate bridge operations as well as repairs and construction not just around the Yankees' schedule but also around the Jets and Giants and special events at the Jersey Meadowlands such as Bruce Springsteen concerts."[1]

Durando and McKee worked together in their previous jobs, Durando as general manager and McKee as physical plant manager at the Holland Tunnel. McKee says, "When something comes up, Bob and I know exactly what the other guy is thinking and what to do." During my hours with them the two Bobs were regularly on their BlackBerrys responding to phone calls and text messages from bridge offices and Port Authority headquarters in Manhattan, which made me feel less guilty about taking them away from their desks.

Bob Durando worked his way up to top man at the George Washington starting out as a temporary toll collector at the Port Authority's three Staten Island bridges—the Goethals, Bayonne, and Outerbridge Crossing. "The culture I grew up in was different," he says. "You started a job somewhere and stayed with it and moved up in the ranks. Young people today jump around from job to job. I wonder if they have the same satisfaction, feel the pride. Every day I wake up and remind myself that I'm steward of the most important bridge in the world."

Bob McKee considers himself "second generation Port Authority." His father was working for the Authority when he was born; later, they overlapped. As he puts it, "I've been in the Port Authority and it's been in me all my life. This isn't just my job." McKee says he works for "MotherPONYA," the second part of which stands for "Port of New York Authority"—the Authority's original name. "We think of the Port Authority facilities as our other mother," McKee says, "and we take good care of her. It may sound corny, but the seven thousand people working for the Authority think of themselves as a family."

Both men love the bridge. Each lives at least an hour away in New Jersey and gets up at 5:00 A.M. to begin his workday. By 6:30 they're at their desks in the G.W.B. Administration Building overlooking the bridge in Fort Lee. Normally they work at least ten-hour days; in emergencies they don't go home. They're on call 24/7. When I've e-mailed them on weekends, expecting to get a response on Monday, they've often answered in minutes via their BlackBerrys. "Yeah, I take it with me golfing," Durando says. When they're not in their offices and something significant happens at the bridge, even if they could handle it from home, they drive in. McKee says, "I tell my staff, 'If you work at the G.W. you're in the major leagues. And I'm the team manager; I've got to be here. If something happened to this bridge and I wasn't here, I couldn't live with myself.'"

During my many visits to the bridge and its offices, I found deep affection for the George Washington and universal pride among the staff. Indeed, those who work at the bridge and, to accept a promotion, must transfer to another Port Authority facility do so with mixed feelings. Steve Napolitano, who served as general manager of the George Washington Bridge from 1997 to 2002 and is now assistant director of the Port Authority's Division of Tunnels, Bridges, and Terminals, says, "People who work at the bridge wouldn't work anywhere else if the choice was theirs. There's a special bond among G.W.B. people. They're like a fraternity."[2]

Ken Philmus, another general manager who had been promoted off the bridge, was driving across it with his wife one day when she said, "Kenny, why are you looking so sad?"

"It's not my bridge anymore," he answered.

"Don't worry," his wife said, "it'll always be your bridge."[3]

Jerry Del Tufo was the physical plant manager at the G.W.B. before he was promoted to general manager of the three Port Authority Staten Island bridges. "I miss the George," he says. "I talked about it so much when I was here that when my mother learned I was transferred to Staten Island she said, 'Whatsamatta with you? You got demoted?'"[4]

Del Tufo and Robert Eadicicco, formerly operations manager at the G.W.B. and now general manager of the Holland Tunnel, occasionally meet Bob Durando for breakfast at the Red Oak Diner in Fort Lee. Afterward, the three men light up cigars and take a just-after-sunup stroll across the George on the walkway before each heads to his present job site. "We're G.W.B. junkies," Del Tufo says. "We can't stay away from the bridge. When I left here, a chunk of myself remained behind."

BOB DURANDO, BOB MCKEE, AND I began our tour of the bridge on the south walkway heading east toward the New Jersey tower. We passed the monument to Bruce Reynolds, one of the thirty-seven Port Authority police officers who died on 9/11 at the World Trade Center and the only one whose regular assignment was the G.W.B. A small contingent of bridge patrolmen was sent down to the site, the rest remaining behind to manage the transportation crisis occasioned by the closing of the bridge and to guard against attempts on the structure itself. A picture of Reynolds is engraved in polished black granite above the legend THE FACE OF A HERO / HE GAVE HIS LIFE FOR AMERICA / YOU ARE IN OUR HEARTS FOREVER. People still regularly leave flowers and flags beneath the stone.

In Fort Lee, Bridge Plaza South, on which the G.W.B. offices are located, has been renamed Bruce Reynolds Boulevard. To get to the entrances to the north and south walkways, you follow the signs on the boulevard down to Hudson Terrace. Toward the bottom of Bruce

Reynolds, just off the south sidewalk, are huge chunks of traprock that are believed to have been blasted out of the Palisades when the G.W.B. was built between 1927 and 1931.

At the New Jersey tower, a security guard unlocked the high cage topped with barbed wire that surrounds the south side of the tower where it passes through the bridge roadway. Despite their positions, Durando's and McKee's credentials were checked as carefully as was the pass they had secured for me. Inside, we stepped into a small rack-and-pinion service elevator. Elevators in the towers? In the innumerable times I'd crossed the bridge I'd never noticed them.

First we descended the tower to the south concrete platform at its base, which at this time was some fifteen feet above the river; at high tide more of the platform is covered. The base goes down about a hundred feet to bedrock. Half of the New Jersey tower rests on this platform, eight giant steel feet bolted to its surface, the other eight bolted to the north platform. While the New York tower stands on rock jutting out from Manhattan, the center of the New Jersey tower is seventy-six feet out into the Hudson.

The tide was running out at that hour. We were under fourteen lanes of rushing traffic—currently 300,000 vehicles per day, 2.1 million per week—yet down below it was tranquil and quiet, the water lapping about the giant platform, and I kept thinking what a splendid place this would be to go fishing.[5] You wouldn't have to worry about the vagaries of a boat or about anchoring in the strong current. You could just throw your line out into the river and let it drift downstream.

My fishing fantasy was set aside when we reentered the elevator and slowly rose through the roadside level and up, up above the tower's great arch, where there is a kind of mezzanine. Dismounting and moving left, we entered another tiny elevator that rises just short of the level on which the saddle rooms are found. Climbing additional levels of steel stairs, we entered the north saddle room.

In each of the saddle rooms in both towers, two of the huge barrel cables pass over heavy steel structures known as "saddles," which support the barrel cables atop the towers. Created on-site, the barrel cables are three feet in diameter, each containing 26,474 galvanized steel wires, spun one at a time across the river. The barrel cables are instrumental to the functioning of the bridge. Attached to them are the much thinner suspender cables, or "stringers," that descend to support the roadway.

Having climbed from their lowest point, fifteen feet above the midway point of the bridge, the barrel cables now begin their descent from the New Jersey tower to the anchorage in the Palisades. The same engineering is to be found heading east to the New York tower, terminating in the New York anchorage.

I had thought the barrel cables must be greased so they could slide back and forth over their saddles, responding to the weather and the number of heavy vehicles traveling over the bridge, but, as Bob Durando pointed out, if they did that they would quickly wear out. The cables are actually bolted to the saddles. It isn't the barrel cables but the towers themselves that flex ever so slightly. Bridge engineers talk about "dead weight" and "live weight." Dead weight is the bridge itself; live weight, the traffic passing over it. The George Washington is built so solidly that its live weight, as bridge staffers are fond of saying, is "like an ant on an elephant's back."

Nevertheless, in one way or another, all of the bridge moves. In hot weather the barrel cables and suspender cables expand; in cold they contract. Thus the roadways may be lower in summer, higher in winter. There are also steel finger joints in the bridge road surfaces that expand and contract horizontally in response to the weather. Bob McKee said, "A suspension bridge like the George either moves or it cracks and falls into the river. A bridge like this doesn't just stand there; it's a machine. It's almost alive."

From the saddle room we ascended one more level to reach the open-air space atop the tower, accessible via a hatch in the ceiling. To get up there we climbed a ladder—not a leaning ladder you'd climb to clean out the gutters on your house, but a straight-up-and-down ladder with thin steel rungs set so close to the bulkhead there was only room for my toes. Designed to take up as little space as possible, it reminded me of ladders on submarines.

Just before reaching the top of the ladder, I banged my head on a steel beam. The cap I was wearing blunted the blow, but not by much. It was my Appalachian Mountain Club cap, which seemed appropriate for climbing up into the sky, even mostly by elevator. I didn't say anything when I smacked my head; I didn't want my companions to think they had erred in inviting me. I had a big lump for a week afterward. My son kept ribbing me, saying, "You growing another head?"

At the bridge summit I found myself on something much larger than I expected, because I hadn't anticipated that here both sides of the tower come together. In form and size the area resembled a tennis court with a parapet around it. Indeed, when the bridge was under construction there were plans to put restaurants or observation decks atop one or both towers, with much better elevators than the ones in which Durando, McKee, and I rode up. A former bridge staff member told me that he once took a Fort Lee dentist and his girlfriend up there and left them alone for a while: the dentist wished to propose marriage in a romantic place. This story made me imagine weddings atop the towers, caterers, champagne—the towers as a site of celebration. There were once even plans for boat slips at the base of the towers so pleasure-seeking patrons could arrive at them by water.

None of this has happened. Now, in a post-9/11, security-obsessed world, and given the steady growth of bridge traffic, it probably never will. For one thing, where would people park on the New York side? But it's nice to dream: patrons could ride up from the base of the towers or access them via the walkways, to dine or just to glory in the view. Having the chance to ascend the towers might make people feel better about the tolls they pay far below.

Atop the bridge tower I felt privileged to be in a place few others will ever see. I felt incredibly free up there. I felt, well, high. At 604 feet up in the sky, you're removed from everyday cares. Bob Durando and I hung over the parapet drinking in the scene—the barrel cables descending at steep angles on both sides, the suspender cables dropping vertically from the barrels to hold up the bridge deck, the unending stream of trucks, buses, and automobiles, from that height resembling miniature toys, the tiny toll booths in New Jersey looking like the starting gates at a racetrack, the deep cut in the Palisades rock through which the bridge levels pass, the complicated spaghetti of cloverleafs and other approaches to the bridge on both sides of the river. From up there everything looked more like a model or a diorama than the real thing. Durando said, "I've been up here a hundred times, and I could come up here a hundred more. If I didn't need the money, I'd manage this bridge for nothing as long as I could come up here once in a while. There's nowhere I'd rather be."

I had the sense Bob McKee didn't exactly share this feeling. He was staying well back of the parapet and looked a little green. "You okay, Bob?" I asked.

"Yeah, fine," he said. "I've just got a fear of heights." This struck me as singular. The man in charge of bridge maintenance, of these very towers—on which a nine-year, $80 million project sandblasting the many layers of lead-based paint down to the steel and resurfacing the towers with material both superior and more environmentally safe was in 2006 just being completed—has a fear of heights.

I had to admire McKee's courage. He approached the parapet now and, holding on, walked around it for some minutes peering down. "What are you looking for?" I asked.

"Potholes in the bridge surface. From up here, better than below, I can see where the road surface is wearing thin. I've got the overall view." Then he added, "Heights or not, anything my workers do, I do. I can even handle walking the barrel cables as long as I don't look down." McKee told me that in July 2001 he'd been offered the opportunity to ride a window-washing unit down the face of one of the World Trade Center towers, and he did it as part of his regimen of fighting his phobia. The man who invited him aboard said, "Hey, this may be the only opportunity you'll ever get to do this." Those words would prove all too prophetic.

Not all of the forty-six men on McKee's maintenance crew mount the barrel cables, only those who are height certified. Some walk the barrel cables when an ice storm coats them, knocking the ice off gradually with axe handles so it doesn't come down in great chunks on the traffic or pedestrians below. When there is a considerable buildup of ice—it can get as thick as three inches—the outside lanes of the roadway, which are almost under the barrel cables, or even the entire Upper Level will be temporarily closed while the ice is removed. "A small piece of ice falling from a great height can kill someone," McKee said.

I asked him why the barrel cables aren't simply wrapped in electrical heating wires that can be switched on whenever there is ice so that it melts. This seemed a better idea than having men walk ice-covered cables whacking them with clubs. "To do it on all four cables would cost millions," he said. "Besides, we did a test section of one of the cables and, when there was ice, turned on the juice. Didn't work. Also, while the men walk the outside cables they can do other things, like replace burned-out bulbs."

Luckily, I have no particular fear of heights, though I thought walking those cables, even if they weren't iced, would have to be an exercise in pure terror. I would one day experience that terror. Just then, I was afraid of something entirely different. There were several huge peregrine falcons in nests not twenty feet away. The last thing I had expected to find atop

The New Jersey tower after the placement of interior lighting in the year 2000. At the center of the arch underside is the opening of the tube in which the giant sixty-by-ninety-foot flag is stored and from which it is deployed. Courtesy of Dave Frieder.

the towers of the George Washington Bridge was wildlife. These raptors make their homes there. Indeed, the bridge staff, in cooperation with the Audubon Society, has provided wooden crates for their nests, placed in steel alcoves that are out of the wind. The birds glowered at me, and I decided it would be better to give them a wide berth. I didn't want one of these things suddenly coming at me, certainly not up here on top of the world. The pigeon feathers and bones surrounding the falcon's nests testified to their hunting prowess. Bob McKee said, "There's nothing quite like a peregrine going for a pigeon. It's like a shotgun blast."

There was another item of interest atop the New Jersey tower: the huge cylinder that, passing through the upper part of the bridge, emerges at the bottom of the arch. It houses the largest free-flying flag in the world. This sixty-by-ninety-foot American flag, ever since 1948, has been deployed beneath the arch on national holidays. The stripes of the flag are five feet wide, each star three and one-half feet across. The original flag, of course, had only forty-eight stars, but flags have to be replaced every few years anyway. The current flag, made of nylon and wool, weighs 450 pounds and can be flown only on days when the wind doesn't exceed fifteen miles an hour—anything stronger would tear it to shreds. Bridge authorities plan to install a weather station at the top of the arch that will indicate the wind speed up there at any given time. For the present, they do their best to guesstimate. An American flag has been tried on the Verrazano Bridge, but the strong winds there, a site so much more open to the sea than the George Washington's, make flying a flag impossible.

It takes an experienced crew of fourteen structural engineers and electricians half an hour to deploy the flag properly and half an hour to stow it. The controls are on the south pedestrian walkway. The flag emerges from its steel cylinder drawn up in the shape of a bat and then is allowed to slowly descend. I know of nothing man-made more beautiful than the scene at night on national holidays when the George Washington Bridge towers are illuminated from within, the green lights on the barrel cables twinkle, and the American flag moves gracefully in the breeze below the New Jersey tower.

There are flashing red beacon lights atop the New Jersey tower as warning signals to aviation, and there are motion sensors as well. Why motion sensors? I wondered. "They would tell us back in the Communications Center if anyone was up here who didn't belong here," Bob Durando said. "We try to anticipate every and any scenario. Say a helicopter lands terrorists up here? Since 9/11, when it comes to security, everything's on the table."

WE WENT DOWN THE VERTICAL LADDER—even more difficult than going up—and the flights of steel steps, and then we took the two elevators down to bridge level. Bob Durando led the way on the south walkway as we headed west and approached another caged doorway, with accompanying security guard and security system, close to where the south barrel cables pass through the bridge deck into the New Jersey anchorage.

We descended into a world quite as unique as the one atop the tower, a vast room hollowed out of Palisades rock. Here, two giant barrel cables enter, and each splits into sixty-one strands three inches in diameter that are tied to the rock. On the north side of the bridge is an identical arrangement. Workmen were down in the anchorage that day installing a dehumidification system to deter cable rust. They were also encapsulating the chamber, isolating it from the porous, damp rock in what one of the men described as "a giant condom." Like an intravenous drip, linseed oil is injected on a regular schedule into each set of sixty-one strands where they emerge from the barrel cables, the oil running down the length of the splayed cable to keep it pliable and to further deter rust.

I asked Bob McKee how long he thought the George Washington Bridge would last if properly maintained. "Probably another hundred and twenty-five years," he said. "At that point keeping things up might be so demanding and expensive it wouldn't be cost effective." That means that the bridge is projected to last two hundred years, because this was 2006 and we were six months away from its seventy-fifth anniversary.

Great skill and wisdom obviously went into building the George Washington. The Pulaski Skyway, the series of cantilever truss bridges connecting Newark and Jersey City over the Meadowlands, was completed a year after the George. It has now been declared obsolete, with plans afoot to replace it. The Tappan Zee Bridge, the most important bridge over the Hudson north of the George Washington, is also considered obsolete, if not dangerous, in need of replacement after only a half century of use. On August 1, 2007, the I-35W bridge over the Mississippi in Minneapolis, only forty years old, collapsed during the evening rush hour with numerous deaths and injuries. It was the seventh American bridge in the past decade and a half to collapse. It is not comforting to know that one out of five extant American bridges is structurally deficient and many others are in serious need of remediation or replacement.[6] The venerable George is not one of them.

Of course, it does require regular attention. "They say the moment we finish painting the G.W.B. we start all over again. Not true," McKee said. "Repairs and touchups are always needed, but we paint the bridge about every ten years, and it takes two to three years to do it. "So much for one of the many myths and legends inspired by the George.

AFTER WE EMERGED FROM THE NEW JERSEY ANCHORAGE, Durando and McKee took me in a van across the bridge into Manhattan, where there is a place for official vehicles to turn around. We parked on hash marks on the Manhattan Expressway facing west, just barely out of the traffic approaching the bridge. I had no idea why we were there. There was a steel door in the long wall next to which we parked. McKee opened it with a key, and we entered yet another strange world, perhaps the strangest yet. I felt like I was following the rabbit down the hole in *Alice in Wonderland.*

We were in what had once been the tunnel that, before the Lower Level of the G.W.B. was added in 1962, carried traffic across Manhattan to the bridge. The tunnel, blocked on both ends, is directly under 179th Street, the George Washington Bridge Bus Station, and the four high-rise apartment buildings built over the Manhattan Expressway, which currently conveys bridge traffic across the island. On the other side of the expressway is an identical tunnel under 178th Street, crowned by the same structures. It once carried the traffic coming off the bridge, most of it heading for the Harlem River Drive.

The 179th Street tunnel was dark, but my companions had flashlights. The dust was so thick we kicked up clouds as we walked. Although these tunnels had only been closed off for forty-four years, they gave the impression of having been abandoned centuries ago. It was as if we were archaeologists who had discovered a lost civilization. I expected any moment to come across a mummy's tomb.

The two Bobs and I walked the length of the tunnel, crossing this narrow part of Manhattan underground. I asked why both tunnels were not opened so as to add another lane to the Manhattan Expressway in each direction, thereby reducing congestion. "We would if we could," McKee replied, "but there's no way we could open the tunnels without the structures above being affected. We may have to do something with them one day, though. Bridge traffic increases every year."

Durando told me that the tunnels have been considered as evacuation sites if a tanker or other hazardous materials truck turned over on the bridge or for people who might have to be isolated or quarantined because of radiation or chemical poisoning or because they were suffering from a dangerously communicable disease. "You could put as many as ten thousand cots in these tunnels," Durando said, "and they would have a self-contained air supply and lighting." I considered that and then thought that, whether such a need ever arose or not, Hollywood would certainly be interested in these tunnels. They are perfect sets for a horror movie. Stephen King would, no doubt, be fascinated by them.

We emerged from the tunnel into bright sunlight, and it took a while for my eyes to adjust. Durando and McKee had one more thing to show me: the little red lighthouse immediately beneath the New York tower. It is in Fort Washington Park, which was designed by Frederick Law Olmsted, the principal landscape architect of Central Park. To get to it, we had to turn around again at one of these places only bridge employees are permitted to access, get off the bridge onto the Henry Hudson Parkway, head south, and, exiting at 154th Street, drive north along the paved pedestrian path through the riverside park. You have an entirely different perspective of the bridge standing by the lighthouse under the New York tower and observing the full sweep of the bridge to the west. The underside of the George has its own remarkable power and beauty.

The lighthouse has a long history. Originally erected in 1880 on Sandy Hook in New Jersey, it was moved to its present site in 1921 and officially named the Jeffrey's Hook Lighthouse. It warned off shipping from the rocky promontory on which the New York tower stands. After the opening of the George Washington Bridge, with its own abundant lights, the lighthouse was no longer needed. The next year, 1932, the lighthouse was decommissioned and essentially abandoned. In 1951 it was on the point of being torn down and sold for scrap. With great public outcry—thanks in part to the already classic children's book *The Little Red Lighthouse and the Great Gray Bridge,* which had been read by countless children and read to countless others by their parents, who joined the cause—a campaign was launched to save it.

CHILD FRIENDS OF SMALL LIGHTHOUSE SHOCKED BY NEWS IT'S UP FOR SALE, the *New York Times* headlined.[7]

The lighthouse was finally given to the City of New York and eventually became a national landmark. It is the only lighthouse remaining on the island of Manhattan. Alongside it, under the bridge, I was reminded of the Gilbert and Sullivan song from their operetta *Ruddigore* about a little flower that dwelt beneath and was sheltered by a great oak tree.[8]

Traffic on the bridge with the New York skyline in the background. Courtesy of Steve Siegel.

2

The George and the Brooklyn: New Jersey and New York

GIVEN MY LIFELONG AFFECTION for the George Washington Bridge, I am not likely to be entirely objective about it. There is more to confess: writing a book on the G.W.B., an author must contend with two eight-hundred-pound gorillas, the Brooklyn Bridge and New York City. The Brooklyn has always overshadowed the George, as New York City has always overshadowed New Jersey. And partisans of the George and partisans of New Jersey—I am both, despite my Bronx origins—may develop a chip on their shoulder about that. Nevertheless, biases and all, I mean to confront those two gorillas.

In magazine advertisements, as a background for New York–based television news, in movies, as one of the key icons of New York City, attention paid to the Brooklyn Bridge has often meant attention denied to the George Washington. Hendrik Hertzberg, in a *New Yorker* article titled "Gorgeous George," argues that this neglect is unjust: "The George Washington Bridge has never really been given its due," he writes. "The Brooklyn Bridge gets all the attention—the Walt Whitman poetry, the Joseph Stella painting, the David McCullough book, the Ken Burns documentary. Still, the George is . . . very beautiful."[1]

Hertzberg certainly has the right idea. As a matter of fact, though, Walt Whitman does not celebrate the Brooklyn Bridge in his poems and only mentions it in one, where it is merely listed as one of many forthcoming modern wonders. (He also makes an oblique reference to the bridge in one prose piece.) Many writers, no doubt including Hertzberg, assume the bridge is central to "Crossing Brooklyn Ferry," but this poem was written long before the bridge was built, and, of course, the bridge replaced the ferry. Still, each spring, Poet's House in New York City hosts its Bridge Walk, during which poetry lovers cross the bridge and then listen to Whitman's "Crossing Brooklyn Ferry" read aloud in its entirety.[2] The mistaken belief that Whitman was absorbed with the bridge is testimony to its emotional pull—so strong that people will make up things about America's great poet in order to associate him with the bridge and thus add to its luster. Poet's House might consider celebrating a work by another poet on such occasions.

Peter Quinn, writing in *American Heritage,* decried the George Washington's neglect in sentiments still stronger than Hertzberg's:

Overrated
When Roebling spanned the East River with the Brooklyn Bridge ... he created ... [an] icon that has been memorialized in poetry, painting, and photography.... On the basis of this one feat, the Roebling name became synonymous with bridge building.

Underrated
While Roebling's achievement was superb, the true giant among the masters of modern bridge building is another immigrant, the Swiss-German engineer Othmar Ammann. Beginning with the George Washington Bridge in 1931, a towering steel structure at once massive and graceful, Ammann undertook a series of projects that knitted together the New York metropolitan area with some of the world's most beautiful bridges.[3]

Before beginning the research for this book, I was very familiar with the Roeblings and their achievements. However, despite my long love affair with the George Washington Bridge, I knew nothing about Othmar Ammann. While he is revered by engineers and architects and those who write books about great engineering achievements, most Americans, and indeed most scholars very much familiar with the name Roebling, have never heard of Ammann. One critic writes that he is today still "an unknown American master."[4] Some people, when I mention Ammann's name, wonder whether I am speaking of someone in the Islamic world currently in the news. His daughter, Dr. Margot Ammann Durrer, tells me that her father was often mistakenly called "Omar."[5] And I remember, with considerable chagrin, that the first time

I googled Ammann's name (I must have left off the second *n*) I sat reading a page or so about Amman, Jordan, before realizing my mistake.

Why are the Roeblings and the Brooklyn Bridge so well known and celebrated and Othmar Ammann and the George Washington relatively unknown and unheralded? Both the Brooklyn and the George were engineering and artistic masterpieces of their day. Le Corbusier, probably the most influential architect of the twentieth century, preferred the George. At the same time, he celebrated both bridges, saying, "Brooklyn Bridge, which is old ... , is as strong and rugged as a gladiator, while George Washington Bridge, built yesterday, smiles like a young athlete."[6] Engineer David Steinman, Ammann's contemporary, expressed similar sentiments: "The George Washington Bridge ... is fast becoming ... the symbol of its civilization. [It] has gripped the imagination of the young just as Brooklyn Bridge did that of its elders."[7]

The George Washington is certainly the most important bridge of the twentieth century. As *New York Times* architectural critic Paul Goldberger has written, "The George Washington Bridge is to the twentieth century what the Brooklyn Bridge was to the nineteenth—a brilliant synthesis of art and engineering that at once sums up a period and spurs it onward. Both bridges leap over space in a way that still causes the heart to skip a beat."[8] Were Le Corbusier's, Steinman's, and Goldberger's ideas expressed in musical terms, the Brooklyn Bridge might suggest classical music—perhaps, with its Gothic arches, even something played on the harpsichord; the George Washington, jazz.

It could be argued that the Brooklyn Bridge deserves more attention than the George Washington because, completed in 1883, it was in use almost half a century earlier. But the desire to span the Hudson River had existed quite as long as the desire to span the East River, and the George might have been built first had the engineering know-how to build such a long suspension bridge been available. Length was the determining factor; there were certainly other suspension bridges before the Brooklyn, several of them built by John Roebling. Indeed, suspension bridges have for centuries been a means of crossing rivers without interfering with navigation, since they eliminate the mid-river supports necessary for nonsuspension bridges. Probably the earliest suspension bridge was a walkway of wood or bamboo attached by ropes or vines to trees on opposite riverbanks.[9]

One reason the Brooklyn gets more attention may be that it is wholly within New York City, the media capital of the world. That wasn't true when it was built: Brooklyn was then its own city, the fourth largest in the nation. It was especially the Brooklyn Bridge, with one end in busy Lower Manhattan, that created the New York City we know today. The George Washington is far uptown and most immediately connects a residential neighborhood of Manhattan with New Jersey.

Paul Goldberger does not feel that the placement of the George Washington need diminish its importance. He writes, "The bridge's relationship to the city is as important as the structure itself.... One of the true symbols of the city, its relationship to Washington Heights should be like the Eiffel Tower's to the 15th arrondissement in Paris, the patron saint of the neighborhood."[10] Note, however, that Goldberger says "should be" rather than "is."

Earlier plans for a trans-Hudson bridge, before Amman's, placed it at various midtown locations. Had the George Washington been built in any of these places, it would have been much more central to the life of New York City and likely as celebrated as the Brooklyn, if not more. Of course, considering the George's volume, midtown would have become a traffic nightmare far worse than it is today. Also, a great portion of Manhattan would have had to be demolished to provide for long and elaborate bridge approaches: suspension bridges must rise to a considerable height to provide sufficient clearance for ships beneath them. Building the George from Washington Heights to the Palisades, that is, from height to height, allowed for minimal approaches and invasiveness on both sides of the river—and in the case of Fort Lee, then almost rural, for virtually no invasiveness at all.

You understand the importance of the approach issue when you walk across a bridge. Since the Brooklyn Bridge extends from a flat area in Manhattan to a flat area in Brooklyn, its approaches are, proportional to its size, quite a bit longer than the George's, and thus it intrudes a good deal on both New York City boroughs. On the Brooklyn, you walk a considerable distance and ascend to quite a height before the waters of the East River appear below, whereas walking on the George is virtually flat and the Hudson appears below almost immediately.

Spanning the Hudson, the George Washington connects New York City not just to New Jersey but to the rest of America. It is perhaps more of a national bridge than a New York bridge, known as well as if not better than the Brooklyn everywhere but in the city. Its being named for the father of our country alone suggests that its trajectory is national, not regional or local. Perhaps its being a national bridge, and stretching between two states instead of belonging to just one of them (actually just to one city), precludes its having a local constituency the equal of that the Brooklyn Bridge enjoys.

It is well to remember that the Brooklyn is only one of nineteen bridges connecting Manhattan with the other New York City boroughs while the George is a monumental gateway not only for those commuting to and from the city but for those arriving in the East after a transcontinental voyage and, as well, those embarking for the West. Heading west on the George Washington, you can instantly pick up Interstate 80 and continue on it all the way to San Francisco. A friend who grew up in New York, Martin Kushner, says that the first time he crossed the G.W.B., at the beginning of a cross-country trip, he felt like he was "entering another country."[11]

Similarly, Herbert Mays, a prominent New York magazine editor, often said, "As far as I'm concerned, the United States of America ends at the Hudson River." Manhattanites, who like to think of themselves as cosmopolitan, may actually be markedly provincial in their certitude that New Jersey—and even the "outer boroughs," not to mention the rest or at least the vast middle of the nation—is of little importance. Some years ago I attended a symposium on American icons, held at Columbia University in Manhattan, where the Brooklyn Bridge was given much attention by the panel of speakers. I asked why the George was not also under consideration. One panel member, to the general merriment of the others, answered, "How can the George Washington Bridge be an icon? Look where it goes."[12] One of my neighbors, Alice Caulkins, says, "New Yorkers have always regarded New Jersey as merely a spiderweb of roads to somewhere else."[13]

This attitude—along with much of the money, power, and status of Manhattan—is concentrated in the island's interior avenues. Manhattanites tend to turn their backs on the city's finest amenities, its rivers. Unlike residents of such European cities as London, Paris, and Budapest, for whom the Thames, the Seine, and the Danube respectively are at the very center of urban life, the waterways of Manhattan—the Hudson, Spuyten Duyvil, the Harlem, and the East River—are largely ignored, and much of the island's least expensive property borders them. Few who live in Manhattan are mindful that four of New York City's five boroughs are on islands, that geographically New York is Venice's cousin. New York actually has far more bridges than Venice, 2,027 at last count.

The parochialism of Manhattanites is burlesqued in the famous Saul Steinberg *New Yorker* cover drawing titled "View of the World from 9th

The bridge shortly after it was inaugurated. Note that only the Upper Level is in place. The New Jersey tower, standing on its two river platforms, is in the foreground. Courtesy of Special Collections and University Archives, Rutgers University Libraries.

Avenue." The foreground of the picture is a street scene in Manhattan. The rest of the world, beginning with a small, dark smudge titled simply "Jersey," is of little consequence. A 1929 *New Yorker* cartoon, with a drawing of the George Washington Bridge under construction, has one workman atop the New York tower say to another, "Yeah, once break the ice wit' Joisey this way and there's no tellin' what'll happen." A recent drawing in the *New York Times* satirizing what it suggests are inadequacies of the Homeland Security Department included the George Washington Bridge and these words: "Expendable: nobody needs to go to New Jersey." For many Manhattanites, the only purpose of the George Washington Bridge is to guarantee their return to the city from places west or north of it, as if it were built solely as a gateway for them. But turnabout can be fair play: the journalist Robert Strauss says that when he wrote for the *Bergen Record*, he and his colleagues would refer to the George Washington Bridge as "the gateway to Fort Lee."[14]

If you've watched New York City–focused *Saturday Night Live* over the years, you've experienced a constant barrage of New Jersey jokes. And Woody Allen's Manhattan-based movies (when they deign to cross the Hudson, it's usually for one quick scene followed by an immediate retreat back across the river) can't seem to do without at least one, such as the comment in *Sleeper*, "A certain intelligence governs our universe, except in certain parts of New Jersey."[15] The attitude of many New Yorkers toward New Jersey, based on an assumption of cultural superiority, is not unlike the traditional attitude of Europeans toward Americans. New Jerseyans in the one case, Americans in the other, are seen as nice enough but not terribly interesting or sophisticated and, thus, the easy targets of ridicule.

New Jersey has traditionally been thought of as second rate, almost a colony of New York from which foodstuffs could be extracted and where garbage could be dumped. In colonial days New Jersey's governor lived in New York City. Until an 1834 U.S. Supreme Court decision, New York insisted its border was not the middle of the Hudson but extended to the New Jersey shore. Before that year, in a small-scale civil war, mid-river shots were occasionally exchanged between New York and New Jersey constables, and New Yorkers more than once sailed over to New Jersey and burned its piers for "trespassing on New York territory." Indeed, as recently as 1998, New Jersey and New York were contesting jurisdiction over Ellis Island. Once again, the Supreme Court had to adjudicate; in a Solomon-like verdict, it declared that 90 percent of the island is actually in New Jersey, 10 percent in New York.[16]

Until New Jersey governor William Cahill complained, when planes landed at Newark Airport flight attendants would say, "We have landed at Newark Airport. Welcome to New York." The Jets and Giants professional football teams both play their home games in New Jersey but call themselves "the New York Jets" and "the New York Giants." For fifty-one years, from its origin in 1921 until 1972, the Port Authority was called "the Port of New York Authority," even though its first original project was the George Washington Bridge and, ironically, the greater part of the port itself—that is, the shipping facilities—has for many years been located in New Jersey. Because of New Jersey dissatisfaction, its name was changed to "the Port Authority of New York and New Jersey." Over the years New York has repeatedly had to be forced to negotiate with New Jersey as equals. Jameson Doig, in his history of the Port Authority, *Empire on the Hudson,* speaks of "the long history of efforts by New York's elected leaders to resist cooperation with its sister state."[17] If the Port Authority had not been created for joint state projects it could easily—its banner displaying the seals of both states—have been invented merely as a device to guarantee a modicum of peace between New Jersey and New York.[18]

Speaking of which, people in our part of the country almost never say "New Jersey and New York." They say "New York and New Jersey," as if New York is the senior partner. I did it the other way around above and in this chapter's title on purpose.

The secondary status of New Jersey in the minds of New Yorkers might explain why the seventy-fifth anniversary of the George Washington Bridge, October 24–25, 2006, was all but ignored in the city while considered a major event across the river. The *Star-Ledger,* New Jersey's leading newspaper, had a front-page story and gorgeous color photographs shot from atop the bridge's towers. It sold prints of these photographs for several weeks thereafter. New Jersey's second newspaper, the *Record,* had a full Sunday section devoted to the bridge, with a host of articles and illustrations, introduced by these words: "North Jersey as we know it was born on October 24, 1931."[19]

In contrast, the *New York Times* ignored the seventy-fifth altogether, giving it not one word, not even in its Metropolitan section or its Sunday New Jersey–Regional section. (New York's *Daily News* did have a short feature on the anniversary.)[20]

No official event whatsoever was held in New York City; both the celebration of October 24 (commemorating the inauguration) and that of October 25 (commemorating the opening) were held in Fort Lee. Mayor Jack Alter of Fort Lee attended both, but his opposite number, Mayor Michael Bloomberg, did not attend either. Moreover, while the governor of New Jersey, Jon Corzine, attended the October 25 celebration in Fort Lee Historical Park and spoke with passion about the beauty and significance of the bridge, Governor George Pataki of New York attended neither celebration. The New York governor and New York City mayor have routinely attended the Brooklyn Bridge's anniversary celebrations.

In my quest to understand why New York overwhelmingly favors the Brooklyn over the George, I interviewed two authors of books on the Brooklyn Bridge, Alan Trachtenberg and Richard Haw. Trachtenberg, author of *Brooklyn Bridge: Fact and Symbol,* feels that "the George Washington is a gorgeous structure, but you generally can see it whole only from a distance. The Brooklyn has an intimate quality and is at the center of things. The George is way uptown, more or less out of things."[21]

There is truth in what Trachtenberg says. To get a full view of the immense George Washington, you have to take one of the Circle Line boats around Manhattan or travel north on the Henry Hudson Parkway in Manhattan or on River Road just south of the bridge in New Jersey. Or you can circumnavigate Manhattan in a canoe, as I once did. Beneath the bridge I examined the undersides of cars and trucks passing overhead, a view you ordinarily don't have of them. The vehicles looked so vulnerable, as if their private parts were exposed. I felt almost as if I should avert my eyes.

The George, as Trachtenberg suggests, *is* almost too big to wrap one's mind and camera aperture around. In saying that the George is "out of things," though, Trachtenberg doesn't take into account its Revolutionary War history and the beauty of its location. For many, this portion of the gleaming and powerful Hudson River, with the Palisades on the western shore and Washington Heights on the eastern, is more beautiful than any other major bridge site in North America. At the time the Lower Level was completed in 1962, these words appeared in a newspaper: "Now for a long way up and down the Hudson and across the island and from many points on the opposite shore, Mr. Ammann's bridge glorifies the landscape by day and offers a sparkling crown to the river by night. One could almost say it would be worth its cost if it were only a monument and no human being or vehicle ever crossed it."[22]

Early names considered for the George Washington included the Palisades Bridge, the Hudson Bridge, and the Fort Lee Bridge, all references to the G.W.B.'s magnificent location. There are reasons why the Hudson gave its name to an important school of American painters. The East River, which the Brooklyn Bridge spans, shows little promise of ever doing so. There is, unlike the George Washington's, nothing remarkable about the Brooklyn's location. It may be that, as the writer Philip Lopate believes, the Brooklyn Bridge is "lovable." I certainly find it so. Its scale—not when it was built and towered over everything but today, when it is surrounded by tall buildings—evokes the charms of Europe. Its broad walkway is largely of wooden planks, and, walking across it, you can touch its stone towers and enjoy the handsome historical plaques displayed there. Still, when it was first built, there were critics, such as Montgomery Schuyler, who celebrated its engineering but regarded the Gothic towers admired today as derivative and dull.[23]

Whatever the merits of the Brooklyn, the George Washington's grand and stately qualities and its relationship to its site are equally worthy of celebration.[24] Whereas the Brooklyn's towers suggest a dark medieval cathedral, the George Washington's suggest a bright contemporary one. Historian James Morris, after considering the Brooklyn Bridge, became a partisan of the George Washington. He writes: "On the other shore of Manhattan stands the George Washington Bridge.... This is a much nobler thing. It stands very high above a much more splendid river and is embedded at its western end in the wooded bluffs of the Palisades—a very different conclusion from the homely clutter of Brooklyn."[25]

Richard Haw, author of *The Brooklyn Bridge: A Cultural History*, would, I am sure, not agree. As Haw wrote to me, expressing sentiments similar to Lopate's and Trachtenberg's, "The G.W.B.'s story is as fascinating as the Brooklyn Bridge's, but the Brooklyn's pre-industrial element makes its story more romantic.... The G.W.B. is a first-class icon to modern architects, but the aesthetics of modern architecture don't always appeal to the public. It's a very handsome bridge (more in its strength, though, than in its beauty).... People love to walk across the Brooklyn Bridge. I'd suspect no one loves to walk across the G.W.B."[26]

There is merit to Haw's remarks. Something in the Brooklyn I miss in the George: its glorious promenade, which is above and separated from traffic and encourages leisurely strolling. Emblematic of an earlier day, more than the George it is made for the pedestrian. However, many people do love to walk across the George Washington, and jog across it, and bike across it, and roller-skate across it. It's hard to deny that the Brooklyn is more romantic, if only because many people find anything with antique qualities romantic. Also, the pathos of the Roebling saga (the father, John, dying from tetanus contracted while supervising the bridge's construction; the son, Washington, assuming his father's role but becoming an invalid after contracting the bends; the son's wife, Emily, heroically carrying his instructions to the workmen he monitored from his Brooklyn apartment window) is a sentimental factor in the Brooklyn's appeal. Othmar Ammann lived to a ripe old age and built many bridges after the George. There is no way to see him, as some tend to see the Roeblings, as a martyr.

Nor has the George itself been steeped in tragedy the way the Brooklyn Bridge has from the beginning. Shortly after it opened, pedestrians fearing a collapse stampeded, and twelve people were crushed to death. A few years ago, an unlucky weekend jogger died when a cable, under great tension, tore loose and decapitated him. On September 11, 2001, thousands fled across it just as the World Trade Center towers came down behind it. These events have added to the Brooklyn's mystique.

I would also take issue with Haw's comment that the George is handsome more because it is strong than because it is beautiful. The George is certainly strong looking. A neighbor of mine, Arline Dodge, admits to being afraid when crossing other bridges but not when crossing the George Washington. "I never worry on that bridge," she says. "It's so massive, so strong, so sure looking that it inspires confidence. It has great presence. I feel safe on the George Washington Bridge."[27]

I think, though, that Haw is creating a false dichotomy between beauty and strength, as if gendering the Brooklyn Bridge, with all its detail—its Gothic arches and fine, woven cables, in short, its decorativeness—as female and the George Washington, in its broad-shouldered grandeur and majestic simplicity, as male. Critic Camille Paglia has expressed similar feelings about the George. She writes, "When I cross the George Washington Bridge ... I think: men have done this. Construction is a sublime male poetry."[28] But the George, as is true of both women and men, is more complex. It is strong and beautiful. Thinking otherwise has had much to do with why Othmar Ammann's bridge has been less celebrated than it deserves.

Atop the Palisades with the first surveying work under way. Bridge designer and builder Othmar Ammann is third from the left. Several publications improperly identify Ammann as the man holding the plans, third from the right. This is William Drinker, Port Authority chief engineer. Courtesy of the Local History Department, The Morristown and Morris Township Public Library.

Othmar Ammann

OTHMAR AMMANN WAS, BY ANY MEASURE, the most important bridge designer and builder of the twentieth century and possibly, as some have argued, of all time. Six of Greater New York's major bridges were exclusively his creations—that is, he both designed them and supervised their construction; and in the case of the George Washington Bridge he also served as "entrepreneur," garnering political support and funds. The other five, in addition to the G.W.B. (1931), are the Bayonne or Kill Van Kull Bridge (1931), the Triborough Bridge (1936), the Bronx-Whitestone Bridge (1939), the Throgs Neck Bridge (1961), and the Verrazano-Narrows Bridge (1964). Another of his projects was the lovely Harlem River Pedestrian Bridge (1949). In addition, Ammann supervised construction of the Outerbridge Crossing Bridge (1928), the Goethals Bridge (1928), and the first tube of the Lincoln Tunnel (1937). He was a key consultant on bridges too numerous to name, principal among them being the Delaware Memorial Bridge (1951), the Mackinac Bridge (1957), the Walt Whitman Bridge (also 1957), and, most notably, the Golden Gate Bridge (1937).

The original design for the Golden Gate, which would have included ugly cantilevered sections and been less stable, not to mention that cantilevered bridges inevitably require mid-river or harbor supports, was radically modified at Ammann's suggestion and in light of the success of the George Washington. The G.W.B. proved the potential of suspension bridges to be radically expanded in length (the distance between towers

39

is considered the suspended portion), far beyond what anyone had previously imagined. As one professional publication put it, "The Golden Gate Bridge is a fact today because the Fort Lee bridge was built yesterday."[1] And as one structural engineer has said, the George Washington "became a benchmark—a standard against which all bridge builders had to now think about their designs."[2]

Ammann's prodigious output was accomplished, in part, because of the uncommon dedication with which he approached his work. In a letter to his mother in Switzerland he spoke of that which "drives one with an irresistible force to work, fight, create."[3] His achievement was even more extraordinary, almost herculean, because, between 1934 and 1939, he simultaneously served as chief engineer both of the Port Authority and, under Robert Moses's direction, of the Triborough Bridge and Tunnel Authority. The Port Authority is responsible for bi-state projects involving New York and New Jersey within a twenty-five-mile radius of the Statue of Liberty. The Triborough Authority, now subsumed into the Metropolitan Transportation Authority of New York City, concerns itself with projects in and between the five boroughs of the city. Thus the George Washington Bridge, between New Jersey and New York, was a Port Authority project while the Verrazano-Narrows Bridge, between Staten Island and Brooklyn, was a Triborough Authority project.

Othmar Ammann was a bridge enthusiast from early childhood. Born on March 26, 1879, in the small city of Schauffhausen, Switzerland, near Zurich, he grew up across the Rhine from it in the town of Feuerthalen. As a boy he was fascinated by neighboring bridges and loved to sketch them, which seemed a natural development in one whose grandfather was a noted landscape painter and whose two brothers became artists. As a youth he was interested in architecture, but because of his fascination with pure structure elected engineering instead. He studied at the Swiss Federal Institute of Technology in Zurich. After graduating in 1902, he worked briefly in Switzerland and then in Frankfurt, Germany, where he helped design steel bridges.

A former teacher, Karl Emil Hilgard, who had himself worked as a bridge engineer in the United States, now showed Ammann pictures of American bridges, including the Brooklyn Bridge, and told him that greater opportunities awaited him in the United States than in Europe. Said Hilgard, "I have seen youngsters in charge of work there which in Europe only graybeards would be allowed to perform."[4] There were so many rivers that needed fording, so many mountain valleys that needed

spanning. And of all the places in the United States, New York, with four
of its five boroughs on islands, was ideal, the mecca for bridge builders.

In 1904, twenty-five years old, Ammann sailed for America, thinking
he would gain some experience, take a look at the St. Louis World's Fair,
and return to Switzerland. As he would later write, "With only an engineering diploma in my pocket and little practical experience, I arrived
in New York. I came here eager to learn in this great country about its
engineering works, some of which were already then staggering the
imagination."[5] Except for an occasional visit to see family and a brief stint
in his native land's army, he never returned to Switzerland.

Upon arrival, Ammann secured work at the first door he knocked on,
that of Joseph Mayer, at 1 Broadway in New York. Mayer built railroad
bridges and, like many engineers of that day, harbored aspirations of
someday spanning the Hudson River, which quickly became an enthusiasm of Ammann's. In Ammann's next job, with Frederic C. Kunz of the
Pennsylvania Steel Company in Harrisburg, he worked on some details
of New York's Queensboro Bridge, then being built by his future
employer Gustav Lindenthal. In 1907, Ammann offered his services to
C. C. Schneider of the American Bridge Company, who had been
appointed by the Canadian government to investigate a disaster on the St.
Lawrence River near Quebec. A nearly completed bridge had collapsed,
taking the lives of seventy-nine workmen. The catastrophe temporarily
undermined confidence in cantilevered bridges and affirmed the efficacy
of the suspension bridges that especially interested Ammann. Within a
few months, he had become, in effect, head of the inquiry. His excellent
work came to the attention of many in the engineering community.

In 1910, he was considering returning to Switzerland when he met
Gustav Lindenthal, America's preeminent bridge builder in the very late
nineteenth and early twentieth centuries. Soon after, Lindenthal would
hire him. Of Austrian birth, Lindenthal had come to America at virtually the same age as Ammann but thirty years before. He believed that
"bridge construction and bridge architecture will be to posterity . . . as
sure an index of . . . our present day civilization as houses, temples, cathedrals appear to us of past ages."[6]

Lindenthal's particular passion was railroad bridges. After the Civil
War, trains replaced steamboats as the primary means of travel, and
trains required bridges. Lindenthal came to attention first as a builder
of bridges in Pittsburgh, which especially needed them, being at the
confluence of three rivers. By the time Ammann met him decades later,

Lindenthal had already served some years as New York City's commissioner of bridges. He had designed, redesigned, and/or built such bridges as the Manhattan, the Williamsburg, and the Queensboro across the East River, the next three bridges north of the Brooklyn Bridge. Ammann served as Lindenthal's chief assistant on the construction of the Hell Gate railroad bridge across the East River, which connected New York by rail to New England.

When the Hell Gate, then the longest arch bridge in the world, was completed in 1917, there was no more work for Ammann, largely because, with America's entry into World War I, funding for big projects had dried up. Lindenthal offered him a post managing the Such Clay Company in South Amboy, New Jersey, which supplied materials for brickmaking and other ceramic products. Lindenthal was a key investor. Ammann had no choice but to accept the post because by this time he had a wife and two children (a third would arrive in 1922).

Ammann had married his Swiss sweetheart, Lilly Wehrli, in 1905 and brought her over to America. By 1921, the family would settle in the town of Boonton, in Morris County, New Jersey, where they were to live for thirty-seven years, from 1921 to 1958. The home still stands at 272 Rockaway Street. Surprisingly, there is no historical marker indicating that a distinguished American lived there so many years. However, in 2005, a new bridge over the Rockaway River, connecting Boonton with Parsippany, was named the Othmar Ammann Bridge. Ammann's daughter, Dr. Margot Ammann Durrer, who grew up in the Boonton house, was at the bridge's inauguration ceremonies as an honored guest.

Ammann was thrilled when, in 1920, Lindenthal invited him to return to work with him on the dream project: a bridge over the Hudson River. In his earliest days in America, Ammann had written to his wife-to-be: "You can well imagine how I enjoy walking along the shore of that beautiful, wide river. [It] made the heart leap for joy.... The shores are very picturesque, similar to those of the Lake of Zurich but much wider, and they rise more sharply and higher—then they merge gradually into natural woods with many romantic places.... Hardly any other large city has such natural beauty in its vicinity."[7]

Ammann became fascinated by the idea of a bridge across the Hudson—almost the equivalent, in that day, of putting a man on the moon a half century later. Years afterward he related how "my first serious interest in the problem of bridging the Hudson" was awakened when walking along the top of the Palisades in New Jersey. "For the first time

I could envisage the bold undertaking, the spanning of the broad waterway with a single leap of 3000 feet . . . nearly twice the longest span in existence. . . . From that moment . . . I followed all developments with respect to the bridging of the Hudson with keenest interest."[8] Actually, the suspended central span of the George Washington Bridge, that is, the distance between the two towers, is 3,500 feet; the bridge's total length, anchorage to anchorage—including the suspended side spans east of the New York tower and west of the New Jersey tower—is 4,760 feet.[9]

Over the years there were as many as twelve proposals for a Hudson River bridge to Manhattan. The first was in 1805, when a floating wooden bridge stretching to Eleventh Street in Manhattan from his estate in Hoboken (where Stevens Institute of Technology now stands) was proposed, though not built, by Colonel John Stevens. In 1868, the New Jersey legislature chartered a bridge company, but no definitive action was taken, partly because it proved impossible for New Jersey and New York to cooperate on such a project. Over the years it would become increasingly clear that without a bi-state agency such as the Port Authority, no projects of substance involving both states would ever be realized.

In 1885, Lindenthal was negotiating with the Pennsylvania Railroad about a Hudson River railroad bridge, and in 1895, ground was broken for just such a bridge, which would have run from Hoboken to Twenty-third Street in Manhattan. But the project languished in the wake of an economic recession. A monument that was to serve as the cornerstone of the proposed bridge can be found today outside the library of the Stevens Institute in Hoboken.

By 1920, Lindenthal, with his newly formed Hudson River Bridge Company, was proposing a bridge from Weehawken, New Jersey, to Fifty-seventh Street in Manhattan. He envisioned a double-deck bridge, with an upper level for sixteen lanes of vehicular and pedestrian traffic and a lower level accommodating twelve sets of rails. Such a bridge would have been enormous. "Imagine," he wrote, "in a central part of New York City, within a stone's throw of its greatest avenue, . . . a massive stone viaduct and lofty columns . . . over blocks of buildings to a magnificent bridge over the North River [a now antiquated name for the Hudson], leaping . . . over its entire width. . . . Then imagine the . . . tracks continued . . . in New Jersey to connections with all existing railroads."[10] Lindenthal's drawings for this bridge included massive towers 840 feet high, taller than any building in New York, including what was then the tallest in the world, the Woolworth Building. The other dimensions of the proposed bridge were also huge. Lindenthal's colossal bridge would have dominated, if not overwhelmed, New York City.

Ammann was at first captivated by Lindenthal's grand plan. He wrote home to Switzerland, "The new project brings me great satisfaction."[11] Between 1920 and 1922, he worked not only on the bridge's design but on creating the political climate necessary in both states to make it a possibility, experience that would come in handy later when he proposed his own bridge. But by 1922 Amman began to see that his mentor's ideas were impractical and that he had more than a touch of megalomania. Ammann could foresee that a giant bridge emptying an immense amount of traffic into midtown Manhattan would create unspeakable congestion. He would one day write an article referring to such structures titled, with a nod to Jonathan Swift, "Brobdingnagian Bridges."[12] Also, Lindenthal's plan focused primarily on railroads, when it was becoming clear by the 1920s that the automobile was the technology of the future. As Ammann would later write, "Today, any bridge across the Hudson River at New York must be viewed primarily as a highway structure, only incidentally accommodating rail traffic."[13]

Ammann repeatedly suggested to Lindenthal that he at least scale down the project, but the latter was adamant. Lindenthal was six feet tall and barrel-chested, a bearish titan of a man. Ammann was only five foot five, slim, modest, and economical in both speech and manner. Lindenthal wanted his bridges not only to be strong but to look strong. Ammann favored a light and graceful look. It was almost as if the heavy bridge Lindenthal wished to build over the Hudson and the streamlined one Ammann would one day build were reflections of their physiognomy.

Ammann, to little effect, proposed to Lindenthal a bridge primarily for automotive vehicles to be built far uptown in Manhattan, from 178th Street over to the Palisades. This was a narrow point in the river, and the rock of Jeffrey's Hook in Fort Washington Park protruded an extra hundred feet into the water, which made it an ideal location for the New York tower just as the Palisades offered itself for the New Jersey anchorage. Also, as mentioned earlier, a bridge built from one height to another would require far shorter approaches and far less disruption on either shore.

In 1923, Ammann again discussed his ideas with Lindenthal, who this time grew angry. In the three-by-five-inch daybook Ammann always carried and in which he noted the major events of his day he wrote,

"Submitted memo to G. L. urging reduction of H.R. Br. [Hudson River Bridge] proposal. G. L. rebuked me for my 'timidity' and 'shortsightedness' in not looking far enough ahead. He stated that he was looking ahead for 1000 years."[14]

Disconsolate, Ammann wrote to his mother in Switzerland: "I will no longer conceal from you that the giant project for which I have been sacrificing time and money for the past three years lies in ruins. In vain, I as well as others have been fighting against the unlimited ambition of a genius who is obsessed with illusions of grandeur. He has the power in his hands and refuses to bring moderation into his gigantic plans. Instead, his illusions lead him to enlarge his plans more and more, until he has reached the unheard of sum of half a billion dollars—an impossibility even in America."[15]

At this point, Ammann had three choices: to remain with Lindenthal in a position he now found professionally unpromising; to return to Switzerland, giving up on his New World ventures; or to leave Lindenthal's employ and strike out on his own in America. Passionate about the Hudson River bridge project, he decided to proceed with it come what may. As he wrote to his mother, "I have gained a rich experience and have decided to build anew on the ruins with fresh hope and courage— and, at that, on my own initiative and with my own plans, on a more moderate scale."[16]

For the next two years Ammann and his family subsisted on savings and on money borrowed from relatives in Switzerland. A friend lent him office space in Manhattan. There he began to design what eventually became the George Washington Bridge and to campaign for its construction. From 1923 to 1925, Ammann closely fit the stereotype of the artist who sacrifices all for principle. He recalls Ayn Rand's character Howard Roark in the novel *The Fountainhead* in his single-minded and uncompromising commitment to a certain architectural/engineering vision.[17] A neighbor in Boonton was often up late attending to her sick mother. Whenever she "looked over to the Ammann house at one o'clock, three o'clock, there was always a light burning in Mr. Ammann's study and I knew he was working."[18]

Luckily, Ammann had a key ally: George Silzer, who had been elected governor of New Jersey in 1922. Ammann had met Silzer during the years he managed Such Clay. Like Lindenthal, Silzer was a shareholder in the company. He recognized that Lindenthal's proposal was impracticable and that tunnels would make better sense in midtown Manhattan.

Indeed, the very immensity and expense of Lindenthal's proposals had given impetus to the building of tunnels. The Holland Tunnel (completed in 1927) was already under construction, and proposals were being considered for another project at midtown that would one day be the Lincoln Tunnel. Tunnels require very little by way of approaches— there is no need to rise to a great height to permit river navigation—and therefore are more useful in center-city areas.

Silzer viewed Ammann's proposal as eminently doable, and he fervently hoped he might one day point to a bridge over the Hudson River as an achievement of his administration. He encouraged Ammann to lobby for his proposal in New Jersey's Bergen County and across the river on the Upper West Side of Manhattan, in the Bronx, and even into Connecticut, and much of Ammann's time between 1923 and 1925 was spent on the road advocating for the bridge. Silzer submitted Ammann's plans to the Port of New York Authority, as it was then called. He told its commissioners privately that Ammann, albeit young and relatively inexperienced compared to Lindenthal, was the best person to build the bridge. "Mr. Ammann is thoroughly skilled in this kind of work," he wrote.[19] He also sent a letter to Julius Henry Cohen, for many years Port Authority general counsel, suggesting that "the Port Authority ought to avail itself of the services of Mr. O. H. Ammann.... I understand that just at the moment he is available."[20]

Ammann was, of course, more than available; he had been awaiting this moment for years. He had, together with Silzer, as one commentator has noted, "carried out a brilliant campaign to have the Port Authority of New York build the George Washington Bridge and to hire him to design it and oversee its construction."[21]

Silzer, as a courtesy, had sent a copy of Ammann's plan to Gustav Lindenthal. Lindenthal was outraged. He wrote Silzer, "Mr. A. has been my trusted assistant and friend for ten years, trained up in my office and acquainted with all papers and methods. But I know his limitations. He never was necessary or indispensable to me.... Now it appears that A used his position of trust, the knowledge acquired in my service and the data and records in my office to compete with me in plans for a bridge over the Hudson and to discredit my work on which I had employed him. He does not seem to see that his action is unethical and dishonorable."[22]

Lindenthal's extreme reaction would be a painful memory to Ammann thereafter, and the two men would never fully reconcile. Ammann was careful to invite Lindenthal to the October 24, 1931, ceremonies inaugurating the George Washington Bridge; Lindenthal rode to the grand-stand in Ammann's car. He was always generous in his public praise of Lindenthal, going so far as to list him as a consultant on the bridge and to regularly pay homage to him as mentor. Now quite elderly—he would die in 1935—Lindenthal still entertained notions of building the giant midtown structure that would have been a second bridge across the Hudson. It is notable that the G.W.B.'s capacity and strength are such that no second bridge has been built between New Jersey and Manhattan in seventy-six years, and none is planned.

Despite Lindenthal's response, Silzer increased his pressure on the Port Authority. It had only been established in 1921 and, except for taking over the construction of the Holland Tunnel, had embarked on no significant projects of its own. Ammann waited. As he wrote to his mother, "The outlook is good, but one cannot praise the day before nightfall."[23] On July 1, 1925, Ammann wrote in his daybook, "Started position as Engineer of Bridges with Port Authority."

In hiring Ammann as bridge engineer, the Port Authority was not only committing itself to constructing a bridge across the Hudson River far uptown but defining the very purpose of the agency. It would take over the direction of all bi-state projects, many of which were languishing, and, instead of contracting all work out, build a large in-house staff. Under Ammann's supervision, construction of both the Goethals and Outerbridge Crossing bridges also got under way, as well as planning for the Bayonne or Kill Van Kull Bridge. With a challenging job and the means of support for his family guaranteed, Ammann became a United States citizen in 1925. His standing at the Port Authority was further enhanced when Silzer, after completing his term as governor in 1926, became its chairman. Now Ammann's talents could shine unhindered by political and interpersonal rivalries.

Ammann was described in these years by one writer this way: "He might readily pass for a respectable Scandinavian sea-captain; there is the same neat blue suit, slightly worn but in careful press, and a coarse-grained, weather-beaten face, deeply lined from eye to jaw. His high forehead is surmounted by a shock of ragged brown hair and his eyes are a faded, distant blue. He wears an old-fashioned stiff collar and carries an old-fashioned hunting-case watch."[24]

Ammann was always professional, always on the job—perhaps to a fault. His daughter, Margot, remembers that each Sunday while the George Washington was being built he would hike with her to a high point in Boonton called "the Torn" from which he could observe the progress being made on the New Jersey tower. But if those Sunday hikes were at least in part recreation, much of the rest of the day was devoted to work. As he wrote to his mother, "Day after day my work called me away from home early in the morning and only allowed me to return home late at night. Sunday brought the welcome relief, in which I could prepare the work for the coming week without being disturbed."[25] If preparing the work for the coming week was "welcome relief," one can imagine what the rest of the week was like. Ammann's dedicated work habits were not unlike those of John Roebling and Gustav Lindenthal—all of them immigrants but literally builders of this country, quintessential Americans.

Ammann's mother, back in Switzerland, worried about him. As he worked on the George Washington Bridge project, she wrote to remind him that spring was coming; she feared that, because of his dedication to his duties, he would hardly notice it. She warned him "not to overstretch your strength. Man can only depend upon his nervous strength to a certain limit and if this is put under too much stress the machine will suffer and the whole organism will get out of kilter. And what then? One is a broken being. . . . Therefore, do not bind your thoughts to your work alone—give your noble being also its tribute."[26]

But Margot Ammann Durrer believes her father has too often been portrayed as being work obsessed, "some kind of wooden goodie goodie. He had a sense of humor and he also had a temper, which would sometimes flare up for minor things in the household that had nothing to do with the moment. When he was angry his pale blue eyes would become steely blue. I remember one time my mother accused him of cheating when they were playing chess. She was joking, but he threw the whole board on the floor."[27]

Ammann was, no doubt, overly precise not only in his work but also in his personal life. After his first wife died in 1933, he married the widow of another Swiss immigrant engineer, Klary Noetzli. While, according to Margot, Ammann loved to garden and "was a romantic, devoted husband who poured affection on my stepmother," he could be very exacting. He once told his new wife, "You may rearrange and run the household as you wish, but . . . the bathroom towels must always hang straight. Never call me at the office, even if the house is burning down; and especially if it is burning down, because there would be nothing that I could do about it."[28]

Quiet competence was characteristic of Ammann. The day before the George Washington Bridge was inaugurated he received a phone

Dignitaries assembled at incomplete New Jersey anchorage carved into the Palisades. Othmar Ammann is in first row, second from left. John F. Galvin, Port Authority chairman, is about to push the button sending the last of 105,684 barrel cable wires spinning across the river. Courtesy of Dr. Margot Ammann Durrer.

call from an army officer asking, "When the soldiers march across the bridge, shall we have them break step?" It had long been gospel among bridge builders that soldiers marching across a suspension bridge should never be in step because this could start ever-increasing oscillations fatal to a bridge. But the George Washington had been built with such strength that Ammann could say with confidence, "That will not be necessary."[29]

On another occasion, when a severe ice storm was breaking trees and bringing down power lines, a panicked engineering student phoned Ammann's house in the middle of the night and told his wife that, according to his calculations, the extra weight of the ice on the cables was jeopardizing the bridge. Ammann said, "Tell the young man to go back to sleep."[30]

On yet another occasion, Ammann was driving across the George Washington Bridge when he suddenly stopped his car and walked along on the bridge. A Port Authority motorcycle policeman rushed up. Recognizing him, he saluted and asked, "May I help you, Mr. Ammann?" Ammann replied, "No, I just wanted to check something out," and returned to his car.[31]

Despite his punctiliousness and reserve, Ammann could show strong emotions. After he heard on the morning news in September 1939 that Hitler had marched into Poland, his wife and daughter found him outside distractedly raking the few leaves that had fallen. In a rare dereliction of duty he told them, "I'm staying home. I'm too upset to go to the office."[32]

In general, nevertheless, Ammann was immensely organized and in control in all aspects of his professional life. Though a triumph, the fact that he completed the George Washington Bridge eight months ahead of schedule was, in a way, a pity. The bridge was projected to be finished in 1932 and cost $60 million. It was completed in 1931 and cost $59 million, one of an extremely rare group of public works finished early and under budget.[33] Given the name eventually chosen for it, the George Washington Bridge would likely have prompted a national, rather than a regional, celebration had it been inaugurated in 1932, for that year marked the bicentennial of George Washington's birth.

"George Washington Bridge" was not an instant choice for the bridge's name. While the bridge was under construction it was known as the Hudson River Bridge. Other names that were mentioned included the Palisades Bridge, the Fort Lee Bridge, the 179th Street Bridge, the Paradise Bridge, the Pride of the Nation Bridge, the People's Bridge, the Bi-State Bridge, the Nation's Bridge, the Prosperity Bridge, the

Rainbow Bridge, the Columbus Bridge, the Cleveland Bridge (President Grover Cleveland had been born in New Jersey and later was governor of New York), the Hendrik Hudson Bridge, and even the Verrazano Bridge. The Port Authority asked the public for ideas. Many school-children and women's clubs responded, and they almost uniformly favored "the George Washington Bridge." This was a key reason why the Port Authority eventually embraced the name, though it briefly considered "George Washington Memorial Bridge" instead.

Ammann's Bayonne or Kill Van Kull Bridge was inaugurated two months after the George. At 1,675 feet it was the longest arch bridge in the world, considerably surpassing the Hell Gate bridge he had helped Lindenthal build in 1917 and not to be surpassed itself until 1977. The fact that all the while Ammann was building the George Washington he was building another record-breaking and beautiful bridge suggests powers of concentration and an appetite for work difficult to comprehend. Either bridge, as one commentator at the time wrote, "might have qualified . . . as an Eighth Wonder of the World."[34]

In 1939, at age sixty, having by then already built the George Washington, the Bayonne, the Triborough, and the Whitestone bridges and consulted on numerous others, and having spent fourteen years with either or both the Port Authority and the Triborough Authority, Ammann left public service to go into private practice. Some feel that he did this partly to put some distance between himself and Robert Moses at the Triborough Authority, who had a tendency to draw Ammann into unwanted political controversies.[35] He would, however, continue accepting assignments from both authorities on a freelance basis, including the Throgs Neck Bridge, the Lower Level of the George Washington Bridge, and the Verrazano-Narrows Bridge. Whereas the Port Authority, under Ammann's direction, had built three bridges connecting Staten Island with New Jersey, it was not until the Verrazano-Narrows was built that Staten Island traffic could connect directly with the rest of New York City without pursuing some roundabout route.

At first, Ammann's new firm consisted only of himself, his son Werner, who had also become an engineer, and two secretaries. As commissions rolled in, the firm rapidly expanded. In 1946, Ammann and Charles Whitney, a specialist in thin-shell concrete design, joined forces and created a huge engineering firm with offices around the world.

Though reduced in size, Ammann and Whitney still exists today in Manhattan. Among its best-known modern projects have been the restoration of the Statue of Liberty and the United States Capitol dome and the construction of Eero Saarinen's magnificent TWA building at Kennedy Airport. Edward Laing has been with the firm since 1951. "We don't call ourselves engineers," he told me, "we call ourselves engineer-architects," and he added, "Because of Ammann we're best known as builders of bridges." Laing remembers Ammann as polite but formal, "not big on small talk. He never came to work without a coat and tie. People around here still refer to him as Mr. Ammann."[36]

Approaching eighty years of age, Ammann gave up his home in Boonton because of the long commute and took an apartment on the thirty-second floor of the Carlyle Hotel in Manhattan. From there he could see all of his New York area bridges, keeping a fine telescope for this purpose. The George Washington remained his favorite. As his wife Klary explained, "That bridge was his first born, and it was a difficult birth. He'll always love it best."[37] Ammann and his wife had the habit, whenever approaching the George Washington, of bowing slightly and saluting the bridge.

The Verrazano-Narrows Bridge, stretching across the entrance to New York Harbor, was Ammann's last major project, and in one sense the city's as well: since the Verrazano in 1964, New York has not built a single major bridge. Like the George Washington, the Verrazano, with a suspended center span of 4,260 feet, was the longest in the world when completed, surpassing the Golden Gate's 4,200 feet of suspension. This time Ammann built both levels of the bridge at once, saving money in the long run and also guaranteeing the bridge would be stiff enough against the wind right from the start, important in that open passage between Staten Island and Brooklyn.

It is noteworthy that none of Ammann's bridges, even the ones on which he consulted, have ever suffered any structural damage or been in jeopardy. "I have been lucky," he once said. "Lucky!" his wife protested, attributing his success to his genius. "Lucky," Ammann insisted in his always modest way.[38]

At the inauguration of the Verrazano on November 21, 1964, tycoon Donald Trump, then a college freshman, was in attendance with his father and noticed all the politicians soaking up attention while the little man responsible for creating the bridge remained inconspicuous. Robert Moses had arrived in the motorcade's first car, Ammann in the eighteenth. Years later, Trump recalled the occasion: "The rain was coming down for hours while all these jerks were being introduced and praised. But all I'm thinking about is that all these politicians who opposed the bridge are being applauded. Yet, in a corner, just standing there in the rain, is this … 85-year-old engineer who … designed the bridge, who poured his heart into it, and nobody even mentioned his name."[39]

Trump's last comment is accurate in fact but requires amending. The self-congratulatory glad-handing of the politicians did halt momentarily when Robert Moses, chairman of the Triborough Bridge and Tunnel Authority, asked Ammann to stand and said, "Friends, I ask that you now look upon the greatest living bridge engineer, perhaps the greatest of all time."[40] Although Moses did not mention Ammann's name, he probably would have had he understood that while he knew Ammann well, having worked with him for many years, others, partly because of Ammann's self-effacing ways, did not.

Later that day, Ed Sullivan phoned Ammann's home to ask if he would be willing to appear the next evening on his variety show, then the most watched program on American television. The Beatles had come over from England to appear on it earlier that year. Ammann, always passionate about his work but never seeking the limelight, couldn't imagine doing such a thing. "Tell him 'No, thank you,'" Ammann told his wife. Then he turned to the others in the room and asked, "Who's Ed Sullivan?" As one commentator has said of him, Ammann "would not have fit into the age of the soundbite."[41]

Several months later, President Lyndon Johnson awarded the National Medal of Science to Ammann, the first civil engineer to be so honored. Earlier, in 1952, the United States Post Office issued a three-cent stamp picturing both a wooden covered bridge and the George Washington Bridge, commemorating the one-hundredth anniversary of the American Society of Civil Engineers.

Over the years, however, the Swiss have done better at celebrating the achievements of their native son. In 1930, while the George Washington Bridge was still under construction, Ammann's alma mater, the Swiss Federal Institute of Technology, awarded him an honorary degree. Albert Einstein was similarly honored in the same ceremony. In 1979, the centennial of Ammann's birth, Switzerland issued a postage stamp with his picture.

Ammann never retired. As his daughter told me, "He was often on the verge of retiring, but there was always another bridge." He built bridges until he died in 1965. Someone once asked him: if you came back to earth in another form, what would it be? "An eagle," he replied.[42] That seems appropriate for a man who loved to build things that soared.

The two towers at the same stage of development. Courtesy of the Port Authority.

4

Building the Bridge

IT IS SURPRISING THAT CITIZENS of New York and New Jersey put up so long with the lack of a bridge over the Hudson, but the river for centuries seemed an impassable moat. There were sometimes waits in Manhattan and in New Jersey of five or six hours for a ferry, and ice occasionally precluded any kind of passage over the river in winter. Foodstuffs spoiled. There were coal famines in New York City. The George Washington Bridge changed all that.

In 1925, the same year Ammann was named chief bridge engineer of the Port Authority and began to build a staff, both New Jersey and New York passed legislation authorizing a Hudson River bridge. But it was not until 1926 that each state came through with its promised $5 million loan to the Authority ($1 million a year for five years) and bonds were issued for $50 million more, for a total budget of $60 million. Toll revenues, it was assumed, would be sufficient to pay off these debts. It was soon clear they would be. In its first year of operation the George Washington Bridge collected tolls from 5,510,000 vehicles. Today, with over 108 million vehicles passing over it annually, the G.W.B. produces more revenue than any other Port Authority facility, considerably more than the three Staten Island bridges—the Bayonne, Goethals, and Outerbridge Crossing—combined. One reason for the great esprit among George Washington Bridge staffers is that their facility supports itself and even other Port Authority facilities and new projects so handsomely. It is a prestigious place to work.

From its financing in 1926, only four years and eleven months passed until the bridge's inauguration. It took considerably less than half as long to build the George as to build the Brooklyn. But after the bridge was financed, there was another step before work could proceed: bridges over navigable waterways require the approval of the Defense Department (the War Department in 1926), which assures that they are sufficiently elevated to permit the passage underneath of military ships with their high superstructures and towering aerials. Suspension bridges are almost always best in these circumstances because they can easily, and often must, be built to rise to great heights and have no mid-river supports to interfere with navigation.[1] In early November 2007 a huge tanker crashed into the midharbor supports of the San Francisco–Oakland Bay Bridge, spilling immense quantities of oil that despoiled many miles of California beaches and coastline and killed great quantities of wildlife.[2] Thus suspension bridges provide certain ecological safeguards as well.

The suspension bridge is, in general, the structure of choice for lengthy bridges. As Ammann would later write, it "is . . . eminently suited for long spans. . . . What would be the maximum practical length? . . . The answer to this depends on the quality of steel." By the 1920s, Ammann had at his disposal silicon steel, which was 40 percent stronger than that available before World War I. With that steel, he felt, "it would be structurally feasible to build suspension bridges of up to 10,000 feet in length."[3] The world is inching closer to that mark. By 1998 the Japanese had connected the city of Kobe on Honshu, the main island, to Iwaya on Awaji Island, with a bridge whose suspended portion reaches 6,530 feet, presently the longest in the world, and the Italians have had an on again, off again project to connect Messina in Sicily with the Italian mainland whose proposed suspended span would extend 3,300 meters, essentially the limits Ammann envisioned. In 1934 the *New Yorker* quipped, "It's a pity Ammann can't live another 100 years. For then he'd build a bridge across the ocean."[4]

On September 27, 1927, in simultaneous ceremonies, ground was formally broken for the George Washington on both sides of the Hudson and speeches were delivered midstream on the steamer *DeWitt Clinton*. Work began immediately on the foundations for the great towers. Creating the single New York tower foundation would be a relatively simple matter, basically smoothing out the rocky surface of Jeffrey's Hook, the promontory of Manhattan schist sticking out into the Hudson that is ten to twelve feet above mean high water. The two New Jersey tower foundations would be far more complicated: they had to be erected out in the Hudson River, because the Palisades descend directly to the river's edge. Had this not been the case, it is likely that the suspended portion of the George Washington Bridge would have been even longer than 3,500 feet.

As early as December 12, 1927, work was proceeding at a rapid pace on the foundations for the New Jersey tower. As Ammann would write his mother, "We are already working 75 feet below the water level. Until now, everything has progressed as planned and all the constructions are further ahead than anticipated."[5] One reason things were going so well is that giant steel coffer dams were being utilized to create the forms for the New Jersey tower foundations instead of the caissons used in the construction of the Brooklyn Bridge. Unlike caissons, coffer dams were not pressurized, so the bends was not an occupational hazard.

Nevertheless, on December 23, disaster struck. The coffer dam for the New Jersey tower's north foundation, receiving the full pressure of the Hudson River, buckled and three men drowned. Until the tragedy the north coffer dam had been considered so inviolable that only a small pump had been thought necessary to keep river leakage into the dam at a manageable level. It is fortunate the accident happened early in the day. Later on, there would have been many more men inside the coffer dam.

In all, twelve men died in building the George Washington, including one when an explosive charge improperly placed in Palisades rock went off prematurely, but the deaths in the north coffer dam received the greatest amount of publicity and are likely the origin of a legend about the bridge I have heard regularly: that during the pouring of the immense quantity of concrete that forms the New York anchorage, on the other side of the river, three workers fell in and were entombed forever. People knowing I was writing this book often would say to me, "Of course, you already know about the men buried in the wet concrete of the New York anchorage, right? They couldn't get their bodies out, so they left them in there." Others told me with great authority that it wasn't workers but the bodies of assassinated Prohibition-era gangsters that were routinely deposited in the wet concrete of the developing New York anchorage. These stories are so pervasive that one young man, William Meredith, wrote a poem inspired by them titled "The Cemetery Bridge."[6]

"Urban folklore!" Bob Durando, general manager of the G.W.B., says, and my research confirms his statement. The legend seems to have originated in the tall tales staff working on the bridge enjoyed telling. Samuel Owens, a young engineer working under Othmar Ammann's supervision, once said in an interview: "A lot of reporters from the New York papers would come up to the bridge to look for stories.... They believed anything we told them. They wanted to know how many men were buried in the New York anchorage.... We'd tell them so-and-so and so-and-so. Actually nobody's buried in there."[7]

After the December 1927 tragedy, the north coffer dam for the New Jersey tower was rebuilt, doubling the steel on the upstream side. With it as a form, concrete was poured down through seventy feet of water and thirty feet of silt to reach bedrock. Multiply its length and width of ninety and eighty feet respectively by the hundred feet of its depth, and that's a lot of concrete. Soon after the north platform was complete, the south coffer dam was completed and the concrete for it poured without incident.

The foundations on both sides of the river were the first of six steps in the building of the bridge. Though several steps can proceed simultaneously, this order is typical for suspension bridges: tower foundations; towers; anchorages; the major, or barrel, cables; the suspender, or stringer, cables; and, finally, the roadway.

Chief engineer of a bridge is a position very similar to that of an army general. The engineer has his "officers" (assistant engineers) and regiments of workers. Coordination is essential so that the various steps in construction of the bridge proceed without unnecessary delays. Materials must be ordered and delivered on time, workers must be trained and available to utilize these materials on arrival, connections between the various parts of the suspension bridge must be made quickly at appropriate times, and safety precautions must be observed. Ammann's ability to keep a thousand details in his head and his calm demeanor made him ideal for such work. It is almost incomprehensible that he could design and build the G.W.B. while simultaneously building another bridge of his design, the Bayonne or Kill Van Kull Bridge, completed just after the George Washington in late 1931—not to mention also supervising the construction of two bridges not of his design, the Goethals and Outerbridge Crossing bridges, both completed in 1928. If Amman was a "general," he was one simultaneously directing fighting on four different fronts.

Once the foundations of the George were in place, the tower footings had to be bolted to them, sixteen for each tower. With these mounted, the towers themselves could rise; although they seem to be single, unified units, each is made up of sixteen columns of steel. Preassembled sections were floated to the work sites on barges, and since the towers were erected simultaneously, heavy machinery and large crews of workers had to be available at both sites. The erection of the towers began in June 1928, with a friendly competition between those building the New Jersey tower and those building the New York tower as to who would finish first. Nine or ten teams of four riveters each worked on assembling each tower. Taking one year and over one million rivets to assemble, the towers were completed by June 1929.

The anchorages followed. The anchorage is where a suspension bridge is tied to the earth, the way one end of a volleyball net is staked to the ground. An unusual feature of the George Washington is that it has only one visible anchorage: its New Jersey anchorage is carved into the Palisades. The New York anchorage, in Fort Washington Park, just west of Riverside Drive, is, in effect, a "Palisade" of concrete created so that the bridge's four barrel cables could be anchored in exactly the same way they are anchored in the Palisades. The New York anchorage is 200 feet across, 300 feet long, and 205 feet high. Consisting of 110,000 cubic yards and 400,000 tons of concrete, it was, when built, the largest concrete structure in the world.

Next the four huge barrel cables had to be laboriously strung across the towers wire by wire, passing over the giant saddles in each tower and then being tied down in the anchorages. It took almost a year to methodically build the four main cables, each three feet in diameter. To carry out the process of what Ammann called "aerial spinning," footbridges between the towers had to be built and pulleys mounted on them over which the wires, only 0.196 inch in diameter, could move smoothly. Spliced into a continuous loop, 434 wires made up a strand three inches in diameter, and there were 61 strands in each barrel cable. If the 26,474 wires in each of the four barrel cables were laid out end to end they would, at 107,000 miles, girdle the planet at the equator more than four times and, together with the wire in the suspender cables, or stringers, would extend virtually halfway to the moon.

Once complete, the barrel cables had to be compacted by a machine called a squeezer, which, with a crew aboard, traveled over two barrels at a time compressing them into their rounded shape. Then the barrels

Inside the cavern carved out of the Palisades for the New Jersey anchorage. Courtesy of the Port Authority.

had to be painted, wrapped in fine twice-galvanized wire, and painted again. The National Museum of American History in Washington has in its collection a ten-foot test section of a G.W.B. barrel cable, complete with one of the cable bands to which suspender cables were attached. The fact that just ten feet of a barrel cable weighs 34,000 pounds gives some sense of the strength and weight of the George Washington Bridge's barrel cables.

Entering the anchorages over somewhat smaller saddles than those in the towers, the barrel cables were splayed out into their sixty-one component strands. These were wrapped around the first of a chain of huge eye-bars that extended deep into the rock or concrete, finally attaching to a steel girder placed crosswise. Concrete was inserted to surround all of this steel in the 150-foot tunnels that were bored into both anchorages.

In the fifth step, suspender cables, hung vertically, had to be clamped to the barrel cables. It is of interest that all of the wire for the G.W.B.'s cables was contracted for with the Roebling Company. Wire for the barrel cables arrived on spools holding twenty-eight miles of wire and weighing 7½ tons. Now no longer building bridges but manufacturing wire for them, Roebling also provided the skilled workers who supervised the spinning of the G.W.B. cables on-site. The town of Roebling, New Jersey, may still be found just off Route 130, immediately south of Trenton. Though the Roebling works are closed and covered over with vines—indeed, are a Superfund cleanup site—the citizens of Roebling live in the row houses that once made up that company town.

Finally, beginning in September 1930, work on hanging the roadway from the stringers began. Like the towers, prefabricated sections 110 feet wide, 90 for the roadway and 10 for each walkway, were lifted by cable from large river barges anchored at all four corners so as to be motionless during the delicate operation. To keep the structure in balance, sections were alternately fastened in place beginning at both towers and moving toward the center and then outward from the towers to the anchorages.

The creation of the roadway was, in some ways, the most problematical aspect of the bridge. For aesthetic reasons, Ammann was determined to build as slim a deck as possible, without ugly stiffening trusses that would have marred its appearance. But with suspension bridges there is always a danger that the bridge can be brought down by wind affecting a thin deck as if it were a sail or the wing of an airplane,

Men operating the squeezer, which is simultaneously compressing the components of two barrel cables into a rounded form. Courtesy of the Port Authority.

making it violently sway side to side and up and down. This is exactly what did happen to the Tacoma Narrows Bridge over Puget Sound in Washington State in 1940. Before it tore itself apart, up and down oscillations of the deck had reached twenty-eight feet.[8]

Ammann was a partisan of what is known as "deflection theory," which holds that as the dead weight of a bridge increases, the stiffening of the deck can be decreased. The George Washington is very heavy, overbuilt for reasons discussed in the next chapter. In addition, Ammann worked out the means of stiffening the Upper Level with steel girders on its underside, thereby not affecting how the bridge looked in profile.

A great deal more work had to be done to complete the bridge, including elaborate sets of approaches on both sides of the Hudson. Land for these approaches had to be secured through often delicate negotiations with local authorities, and property, especially costly on the New York side, had to be purchased. Also, to permit the passage of the bridge roadway, the Palisades had to be cut forty-five feet down, extending 150 feet back into New Jersey. A total of 300,000 tons of traprock was removed. Passing over the bridge from Manhattan or approaching the tollbooths from the New Jersey side, motorists looking to left and right will notice that they are bracketed by Palisades rock. In the late 1950s, further excavation of the Palisades was necessary to create a passageway for the Lower Level and its New Jersey approaches.

It is ironic that Palisades Interstate Park was established, in part, to stop the quarrying of the Palisades. The diabase, or traprock, of the Palisades had been used extensively for gravel in the building of roads in New York and New Jersey and, in giant chunks, to create seawalls to protect a host of New Jersey beach towns. About seven miles north of the bridge is a monument placed by the Federation of Women's Clubs; its plaque celebrates their work to save the cliffs "from destruction for the glory of God who created them." Yet to build the G.W.B. a good deal of blasting of rock had to be done through the southern reaches of the park. We can only speculate whether today, with environmental issues paramount, this would have presented an obstacle to the bridge being built where it is.

History will find it difficult to determine a date when the George Washington Bridge was truly complete. The bridge was inaugurated in 1931, but the center lanes of the Upper Level were left unpaved, and they remained thus until 1946. By then World War II was over; Detroit

Port Authority engineering staff checking on the mountings of one of the towers. Courtesy of the Port Authority.

had reconverted from manufacturing tanks to automobiles, and, with prosperity reigning, the family car became a nearly universal commodity. Traffic on the G.W.B. increased exponentially.

The Lower Level of the bridge would not be completed until 1962 and would have its own inauguration. Ammann had had the foresight to erect such a strong bridge that another level could be added if the need arose. Construction began on the Lower Level in 1958 and never interfered with traffic streaming over the Upper Level. Some thought a second level might cause the bridge to collapse, but it actually made it sturdier. The Lower Level, and the girders between the two levels, acted to further stiffen the bridge so that even hurricane-force winds do not impact the structure. There are those, however, who feel that the slim beauty of the bridge was marred by the addition of the Lower Level, especially because of the girders that connect the two levels. Whatever the truth of this, creating a two-level bridge was an immense novelty in its day and constituted a huge economic saving compared to building another bridge from scratch. Still, since the center lanes of the Lower Level remain unpaved and no tracks have been laid for the mass transit Ammann planned for them, the bridge is still a work in progress.

In retrospect it is something of a marvel that Ammann was able to complete even the principal stages of the G.W.B. in 1931. The stock market crashed in 1929, and by 1931 the great building boom of the affluent 1920s was over. Projects on the drawing board were scratched, though some contemporary with the G.W.B. in the New York City area were brought to completion. These included the New York Central Building that towers over Grand Central Station (1929), the Chrysler Building (1930), the Empire State Building (1931), the Waldorf-Astoria Hotel (1931), Ammann's Bayonne Bridge (1931), and the Pulaski Skyway over the Meadowlands between Newark and Jersey City (1932). But none of these projects held as much promise that the United States would someday recover from its greatest economic crisis as did the George Washington Bridge.

On October 24, 1931, Governors Franklin Roosevelt of New York and Morgan Larson of New Jersey inaugurated the G.W.B. on a reviewing stand placed at the bridge's state-line midpoint. Bleachers were set up for dignitaries, and there were thirty thousand spectators. Bands played. Columns of U.S. Army, Navy, Marine, and Coast Guard personnel marched across the bridge. A squadron of thirty-four planes

Workers up in the superstructure of one of the towers. Courtesy of the Port Authority.

flew overhead in formation, one plane flying under the bridge. The cruiser *Louisville,* below in the Hudson, fired a nineteen-gun salute. The next morning, at 5:00 A.M., the bridge opened for traffic. In anticipation of this moment newspapers had sported gigantic front-page headlines for days, including one in the *New York Times* that trumpeted, "World's Greatest Bridge Links Two States." This was a rare happy occasion during a time of national despair. As one writer has put it, "In the relentless Great Depression, the bridge became a sort of savior in steel."[9]

Franklin Roosevelt addressing the crowd at the October 24, 1931, bridge inauguration ceremonies. Eleanor Roosevelt is seated behind him fourth from the left. Courtesy of the Local History Department, The Morristown and Morris Township Public Library.

The Accidental Icon

ONE PERSON WAS LESS HAPPY than the politicians and the crowds at the George Washington Bridge's inauguration. Othmar Ammann considered his bridge unfinished, naked, undressed. It lacked the stone of the Brooklyn Bridge, and the attitude of traditionalists toward unadorned steel was in 1931 not unlike how many of us regard plastic today. And though steel bridges had been built before, the George did not look like any other steel bridge. It referred to no architectural tradition, in no way evoked the past, was utterly unadorned. Cosmetic plans drawn up for Ammann by the architect Cass Gilbert, whose works included the Gothic Revival Woolworth Building and the Greek Revival U.S. Supreme Court, had been shelved for lack of funds, and, with the Depression deepening, Ammann could not envision when any might be available.

Gilbert's plans included cladding the giant towers of the bridge in a concrete envelope that would be faced in granite chiseled with Beaux Arts flourishes, as well as placing statuary to cover the points where the barrel cables pass through the roadway on their way to the anchorages. In addition, heroic statuary and park-like plazas were planned for both ends of the bridge, with a spectacular fountain on the New York side.

There are those today who believe that had the towers been encapsulated as Gilbert suggested and Ammann desired—an initial outlay of two million dollars—regular painting of the bridge could have been avoided, an immense monetary savings over time. On the other hand, as physical plant manager Bob McKee points out, if the towers had

Engineering World

APRIL, 1926
Vol. 28, No. 4

PROPOSED FORT WASHINGTON-FORT LEE BRIDGE, OVER HUDSON RIVER

Cass Gilbert drawing showing how he proposed to dress the G.W.B. towers in an envelope of concrete faced in pink granite. Note that in this early drawing the Lower Level of the bridge is in place and suspension chain bars are utilized as the main supporting devices instead of cables. The drawing was executed before the contract for spun cabling was awarded to the Roebling Company. Courtesy of Special Collections and University Archives, Rutgers University Libraries.

been clad, corrosion of the steel—inevitable in the salt air of the Hudson estuary—would have proceeded invisibly. Once discovered through X-ray technology, it would have been impossible to combat without, at great cost and danger, removing sections of the concrete and granite, if not all of it.[1]

Of course, had the G.W.B.'s towers been created not with a façade but entirely of masonry, like the Brooklyn's towers, corrosion would not have been a problem. But given the George Washington's dimensions, it would have been near impossible from an engineering perspective and prohibitively expensive. The George Washington's 604-foot towers are more than twice as high, the suspended portion of the bridge between them, 3,500 feet, is almost 2,000 feet longer, and its main cables are almost ten times as heavy and ten times as strong as the Brooklyn's. There are 3,600 tons of cable wire in the Brooklyn, 28,100 tons of cable wire in the George. Were the Brooklyn placed next to the G.W.B., it would look like a toy.

Othmar Ammann had, in fact, hoped to erect a bridge reminiscent in appearance of the Brooklyn Bridge but on a giant scale. A colleague of his, engineer Leon Moisseiff, would write, "For many centuries ... habit saw beauty in the massiveness of stone only. The shadows of the well-proportioned masonry lines of the old Brooklyn Bridge fell upon the towers of the George Washington Bridge."[2] Wishing to think of himself as an artist, Ammann imagined that, without embellishment, his bridge would be considered "mere engineering," especially when compared with the Brooklyn. In this respect, his thinking had not yet progressed significantly beyond John Roebling's many years before. As one historian of the Brooklyn Bridge has written, "By implying that the masonry was 'art' and the rest 'engineering' he [Roebling] seemed to accept without qualification the popular thinking of the age which conceived of architecture as decoration."[3]

Amman entertained similar sentiments early in his career. He was not yet ready to embrace the Machine Age aesthetic of his times, nor to accept the ideas of his contemporary, engineer David Steinman, who said, "I want to preach the gospel of Beauty in Steel."[4] In the final report on the bridge, two years after its opening, Ammann expressed his disappointment that "conditions were not conducive to rendering this bridge a structure of outstanding beauty," and he still hoped its towers would someday be "materially enhanced by an encasement with an architectural treatment" like that Gilbert had proposed.[5] Unintentionally, the George Washington would end up expressing modernism instead of revivalism, with a distinctly Art Deco look to its towers.

Troops marching across the bridge as part of the inauguration ceremonies. Note that middle lanes are not yet paved; they would not be until 1946. Courtesy of the Local History Department, The Morristown and Morris Township Public Library.

Margot Ammann Durrer was as a girl of nine present with her father at the inauguration of the bridge. She told me, "It never occurred to Father in designing the bridge to leave the towers uncovered. Those were the days when gentlemen wore hats on the street and women would not be seen in town without gloves and a hat, let alone bare legs and strapless gowns. Telephones were kept in boxes or out of sight. So towers were meant to be covered!"[6]

Amman was not impressed "by the criticism that the encasement would constitute a camouflage which would hide the true structure and its function. The covering of the steel frames does not alter or destroy their purpose any more than the exterior walls and architectural trimmings destroy the functions of the hidden steel skeleton of a modern skyscraper."[7] The analogy is not apt. A skyscraper's skeleton is of no use to anyone. whereas the "skeletal" George Washington Bridge, has, since 1931, been one of the most useful objects ever built by human beings.

However, in the same final report in which he yearned for an "architectural treatment," Othmar Ammann admitted that the unadorned steel towers had "a much more satisfactory appearance" than he had anticipated, and over time he would come to enthusiastically embrace them and to see, as a colleague of his wrote, that to encase the towers would have been "gilding the lily."[8] Indeed, the G.W.B. would eventually be Amman's favorite bridge. As Margot Ammann Durrer puts it, "He had two daughters, one named 'George,' and I was always competing with her for attention."[9] Ammann's subsequent bridges, without apology, would be built with towers entirely of steel, though clad in steel plating, like most suspension bridges around the world since 1931—making, over time, the purely structural appearance of the George Washington not only unusual but virtually unique.[10]

John Kouwenhoven, one of our finest writers on American aesthetics, felt that, in the long run, it was not just the lack of funds that kept the bridge towers from being clothed in ornament: "The . . . functional beauty of the naked steelwork fascinated people, and there was a widespread popular protest against applying the masonry covering which, according to the original plan, was to be the chief element in the aesthetic appeal of the bridge." The New Yorker went so far as to suggest that the lack of funds was a fortunate circumstance: "Happily for the aesthetic success of the bridge, the stonework would cost more than two million dollars, and this part of the project was suspended. Let us hope that the lack of funds will last long enough to abolish in everyone's mind the notion that the steel should be encased."[11]

October 25, 1931. Opening Day at the bridge, with cars from New Jersey lined up to pay their fifty-cent toll. Note the rock walls of the Palisades through which the roadway had to be cut. Courtesy of the Local History Department, The Morristown and Morris Township Public Library.

An editorial in the *New York Times* expressed similar sentiments: "The monumental design in steel [of the G.W.B.] provides an eyeful that could hardly be bettered by trying to make steel towers look like stone piers." Heralding the opening of the Lower Level of the bridge in 1962, that same newspaper, in an editorial titled "Mr. Ammann's Work of Art," would call Ammann "the dreamer, the artist" and would say: "This beautiful structure ... is as much a picture as any that hangs in a museum.... It is also inspiring to look at, in the realization that when man builds strength he may also build beauty."[12]

Ammann, who was eighty-three in 1962, took great satisfaction in this and the other *New York Times* comments. He had always thought a bridge might be art. In an interview published early in his career, he said, "I am a lover of fine art and I advocate its application to our engineering works of today. After all, art is an expression of our intellectual and moral life."[13]

Some of the world's most distinguished commentators on design were emphatic that the George Washington in particular was a work of art. Le Corbusier rhapsodized over the bridge, calling it "the most beautiful ... in the world, ... the only seat of grace in the disordered city.... Here, finally, steel architecture seems to laugh.... The towers were to have been faced with stone molded and sculptured in 'Beaux Arts' style.... Someone acted.... 'Stop! no stone or decoration here.' ... They dismissed the architect with his decorations."[14]

Le Corbusier's enthusiasm for the bridge is charming, but the noble tale he tells is fiction. No one "acted"; no one said "Stop!"; Cass Gilbert was not dismissed. The bridge as we know it just happened; the beauty many of us celebrate today was an accident. Those who love the bridge must recognize that the appearance of its most prominent feature, its unclad towers, is more the product of serendipity than of design. The complex tower structures, with their massive steel ribbing, are largely a function of the fact that they were meant to hold countless tons of concrete and stone. As one writer has said, "The George Washington Bridge is one of America's most conspicuous unfinished works of architectural engineering."[15] Had Ammann not designed the towers so that they could hold massive amounts of concrete and granite, they would probably have been built in a more slender, less distinctive, and surely less beloved manner. As Moisseiff wrote, "The fact that the towers were conceived to be ultimately encased in masonry is important to an understanding of their design."[16]

One might be tempted to award less credit to Ammann given that the final, much celebrated appearance of his bridge was accidental. The most modest of men, Ammann would probably have been the first to agree. On the other hand, modern art has long embraced the accidental as key to a work's genius, and if credit is awarded to the accidental in a painting—massively so in the case of someone like Jackson Pollock—why not in a bridge? However the George Washington Bridge came to be, it is, as the *New York Times* architectural critic Paul Goldberger has written, "a piece of poetry,"[17] and certainly its builder deserves the credit for that poetry regardless of how it was "written."

Another of the great architects of the twentieth century, Ludwig Mies van der Rohe, was, like Le Corbusier, enchanted by the George Washington, again without knowing the facts behind its uncertain origins. Mies would go and admire the bridge whenever he visited New York. As late as 1963, thirty-two years after it was inaugurated, he was still insisting it was "the most modern building in the city."[18] "Building" is a curious word for a bridge, but Mies was loath to distinguish between one kind of structure and another and between architecture and engineering. He was "fond of the bridge," one architectural critic would write, "because he considered it beautifully proportioned and because it did not conceal its structure. Mies liked to see steel, brick, concrete . . . show themselves rather than be concealed by ornamentation."[19]

The George Washington thus became an early example of what modernists consider architectural honesty. We see examples of this everywhere. The Pompidou Center in Paris, with all of its systems external to the building, is one. A classroom in which I regularly teach at Rutgers University, where the heating vents and plumbing, rather than being hidden in the walls or ceiling, are brightly painted and exposed as articles of ornamentation, is another.

The views of America's greatest architect, Frank Lloyd Wright, on the George Washington Bridge are unknown—perhaps because the egotistical Wright rarely expressed opinions on the works of others except when disparaging them. Still, it is clear that the bridge, with no effort to cover over or embellish how it works and what it is, is a prime example of Wright's central idea, and his mentor Louis Sullivan's, that form should follow function. The George Washington looks like what it *is* and what it *does*.

John Kouwenhoven certainly saw it that way. He chose a photograph of the George Washington Bridge for the cover of his 1948 book, *The Arts in Modern American Civilization*. This work focuses on the struggle in American aesthetic history between the "genteel" or "cultivated" tradition (which he identified with Europe) and an aesthetic of our own, which he termed "the vernacular." The vernacular, examples of which include Shaker chairs and clipper ships, subscribes to Wright's ideas, including doing without frills or decoration not germane to structure and not disguising function. Kouwenhoven, referring to Ammann's 1928 *First Progress Report*, celebrated the bridge because it was "purely vernacular in origin, dictated, as the Report said, solely 'by engineering requirements.'" But Kouwenhoven deplored the report's insistence on " 'careful architectural treatment and a dignified appearance'" in the towers, anchorages, and approaches because "it was here, especially in the towers, that the cultivated tradition would be called upon to create the beauty which it was assumed the vernacular alone could not achieve."

Kouwenhoven saw the George Washington Bridge "as one of the most beautiful structures in America" and "a symbol of our civilization." In effect, he considered it the first great truly American bridge. (It is worth noting that Kouwenhoven never mentions the Brooklyn Bridge in his book. Perhaps he felt that its allusions to the past and to Europe, especially in the Gothic arches of its towers—so reminiscent of those adorning Notre Dame Cathedral in Paris—disqualified it as an example of the vernacular.) He warned against what he considered the false dichotomization of engineering and architecture and called for "a dispassionate study of the relationships" between them. His idea was that Americans, still under Europe's cultural thrall, should struggle against their dichotomization of the useful and the beautiful. He felt that America's genius lies in creating objects whose utility and beauty are inseparable. A bridge, if built honestly—that is, with simple vernacular principles—could also be sculpture.[20]

Othmar Ammann occasionally expressed similar views. Very early in his career, long before he built the George Washington Bridge, he wrote: "Engineering structures are still regarded by many engineers as mere works of utility, which deserve no consideration in architectural or artistic treatment. So long as this opinion prevails, the engineering profession will not lift itself to a higher plane, and it is even running the risk of being relegated to second place—or after the architect—in the creation of such monumental structures as properly belong in its domain."[21] A *New Yorker* article that came out shortly after the G.W.B.'s inauguration dramatizes the issue: "The George Washington Bridge now marks high water in current architecture. This statement is something of a paradox, for the bridge is sheer engineering, and such architectural treatment as has been planned for the bridge proper would probably only take away from its present beauty."[22] Ammann always resisted the stereotype of the engineer as a pedestrian type with a slide rule in hand and a multitude of ballpoint pens inside a pocket protector in his white, ill-fitting, short-sleeved shirt. He said that some might think engineers "lack glamour and sparkle. We might even be considered dull by many people, but I don't believe it."[23]

If routinely dichotomizing the works of engineers and architects may be false, setting artists on the one hand and engineers and architects on the other may also be. Architect Philip Johnson considered Frank Lloyd Wright "the greatest artist America has produced," and the architectural critic Robert Campbell wrote, "America's other great artists—our painters, sculptors, composers—don't really rank with the tops of all time. They're not Rembrandt or Michelangelo or Beethoven. Wright alone has that standing."[24] Frank Lloyd Wright's works, as well as Othmar Ammann's George Washington Bridge, are compelling examples of why a narrow aesthetics that sees structure and art as foreign to one another deserves to be abandoned. Otherwise, engineers risk being thought of as concerned only with utility, architects risk being thought of as mere decorators, and artists risk being thought of as having no particular utility.

If I had to choose the greatest artist of today, it would be Santiago Cala-trava, the brilliant Spanish architect-engineer, who builds exquisite bridges, buildings, and monuments that are not only useful but simultaneously sculptures reminiscent of Brancusi's. Were they smaller, they would probably be housed in museums. As New York–based architect Leslie Feder has put it to me, "The word 'artist' certainly would apply to Calatrava, as to Roebling, to Eiffel, and to Ammann. Engineering, architecture, and art, under ideal circumstances, can be a seamless whole."[25] The critic Beatrice Wood, in defending as art Marcel Duchamp's famous 1917 Dada urinal, insisted that "the only works of art America has given are her plumbing and her bridges." [26] Like Kouwenhoven, Feder would not go that far, but he probably would suggest that we not automatically rule out plumbing's potential as art—and certainly not that of bridges.

Obviously, it could be argued that what is being discussed here is good design, not art; that it is the special province of art to present not reality but alternate realities; that life and art, while reflecting one another, are separate entities. This, while incontrovertible in its own terms, seems to me to also be unnecessarily narrow and limiting. Surely great literature is not confined to fiction and poetry; there is art in the best journalism and scholarship. In the graphic arts, Andy Warhol's Campbell soup cans and Brillo boxes may be regarded as an attempt to not only make fun of but wipe out such absolute distinctions.

When Othmar Ammann died, John M. Kyle had this to say about his onetime predecessor as chief engineer of the Port Authority: "On September 24, the master builder of them all died at the age of 86, leaving as a legacy to the Port of New York bridges which bejewel our city as the churches of Michaelangelo do the city of Florence."[27] Are Michelangelo's paintings and sculptures necessarily superior to his architecture as art, or is it only certain prejudices, and a kind of elitism, that rank the arts as to how "fine" they are? Kyle may have been exaggerating, in an excess of emotion and affection, but then it all depends on how you define "artist" and whether you are willing to think of bridges and architecture as art.

Americans often have difficulty imagining that something useful may also be beautiful and vice versa. Is art only that which hangs on museum walls? The *New York Times* stated that it was in full agreement with Robert Moses at the time of the Verrazano-Narrows Bridge's inauguration that the bridge would prove to be "a masterpiece . . . second only to the works of Shakespeare in the durability of its beauty."[28] Surely engineers and architects have the same potential for evoking feelings of the sublime as do poets and painters.

Three years after Ammann's death the president of the International Association of Bridge and Structural Engineering, Fritz Stüssi, delivered a paper titled "From Leonardo da Vinci to Othmar H. Ammann." In it he spoke of a "line running from Leonardo's first creative idea on the science of suspension bridges to the most perfect realization in our time by Othmar Ammann." When most people consider Leonardo da Vinci, they think of the *Mona Lisa* and *The Last Supper.* But in most of his work Leonardo was not a painter but a gifted inventor, specifically, a civil engineer who, among other things, designed bridges. Stüssi concluded his remarks by insisting that just as the great artist Leonardo was also an inventor and an engineer, Ammann the great bridge builder was also an artist.[29]

There is no question that aesthetics, not just utility, was always on Ammann's mind. As he would write in his elegant prose, remarkable in someone whose first language was not English, and because this was very early in his career in America, "A great bridge in a great city, although primarily utilitarian in its purpose, should nevertheless be a work of art."[30]

Robert Moses is not often celebrated for his artistic sensitivity, but he described Ammann as "a master of suspension and a builder of the most beautiful architecture known to man, a combination of realist and artist rarely found . . . a dreamer in steel."[31] The George Washington Bridge places narrow categorization in question. It is the busiest, and possibly the most useful, bridge in the world, yet it is a work of art. Though its appearance may be something of an accident, it is no less an important icon of American civilization.

Crossing the bridge into Manhattan with traffic backed up by the Cross Bronx Expressway. Courtesy of Steve Siegel.

6

"The Martha" and the Bus Station

I HAD BEEN WORKING ON THIS BOOK for some time when, at a party, a friend asked, "Will you be including a chapter on 'the Martha'?"

"The what?" I asked. I already knew that one of Fort Lee's major streets, which leads to the bridge, is Martha Washington Way. I couldn't imagine that this fact would be worth more than a brief mention.

My friend laughed. "You don't know about 'the Martha'?" he said, incredulous, and told me that when he was growing up in New Jersey the boys in his neighborhood would always refer to the Upper Level of the George Washington Bridge as "the George" and the Lower Level as "the Martha." "I learned about sex from that bridge," he said. A woman at the party chimed in with "Sure, we girls always called it 'the Missionary Position Bridge.'" Yet another person at the party added that he remembered distinctly the traffic reports that would say, "There's a thirty-minute wait for the George, only ten for the Martha. Better take the Martha." Traffic reports no longer say this. Perhaps "the George" and "the Martha" were judged to be sexist or otherwise not appropriate for radio or television. If so, our language is the poorer for it.

At the party, everyone seemed to know about "the George" and "the Martha" but me. When I mentioned that some engineers believe the G.W.B. is built so strongly it could hold up a third level, one of my friends replied, "Yep, that would be 'the Baby.'"

I discussed "the George" and "the Martha" with general manager
Bob Durando. I had feared he might, for propriety's sake, deny that
anyone on the staff had ever heard of this amusing aspect of the
bridge. "Certainly when the discussion is brought up by others,"
Durando said, "the sexual connotation of George being on top of
Martha is acknowledged, but we at the bridge do not refer to the
Lower Level as 'Martha.' We refer to 'Lower Level East' or 'Lower
Level West.' Same thing on the Upper Level." But then Durando, who
is a good sport with a fine sense of humor, added, "But we're creative
people here at the bridge, Michael, and given our preference we'd
rather have Martha on top."[1]

I also discussed, a bit embarrassed, "the George" and "the Martha"
with Margot Amman Durrer. I asked her if she had ever heard of these
terms. She had, and she wasn't embarrassed at all. A retired doctor of
obstetrics and gynecology, she said, "Gus [her husband, now deceased]
and I were trying to shield Father from hearing this sexual joking
about his bridge. He was, after all, pretty straitlaced, a Victorian.
Then, one day, we overheard him telling a joke using 'the George' and
'the Martha' and we knew we needn't stand guard over the Lower
Level's 'reputation' anymore."[2]

The Lower Level of the G.W.B. was inaugurated on August 29,
1962, thirty-one years and many more Othmar Ammann bridges after
the opening of the George Washington Bridge. Governors Nelson
Rockefeller of New York and Richard Hughes of New Jersey were
driven from their respective states onto the Lower Level in convert-
ibles of 1931 vintage that recalled the original inauguration. The large
crowd that greeted them at the state-line midpoint of the Lower Level
stood thirty-eight feet below where the 1931 festivities took place.

In his remarks, Rockefeller said, "Like millions of others, I have
come to regard this great structure as an old friend. I have crossed it
many times; I have noticed its great beauty many more." Hughes's
remarks included these words: "We open ... in effect a second George
Washington Bridge"—which is almost accurate: the six new lanes on
the Lower Level increased the bridge's capacity by 75 percent. Then
the two governors coaxed the always modest eighty-three-year-old
Othmar Ammann out of the stands and grasped his hand together,
flashbulbs popping. Behind the three men was a large photograph of
the G.W.B., and in front of that a bronze bust of Ammann by the

Inauguration of the Lower Level in 1962, with Governors Hughes of New Jersey and Rockefeller of New York grasping Ammann's hand. The bust of Ammann is now in the George Washington Bridge Bus Station. Courtesy of the Port Authority.

sculptor Wheeler Williams that had just been unveiled. Said Ammann, "I accept it with humility, but with a certain embarrassment, because it is not usual that an honor of this kind is conferred on a man during his lifetime." At the conclusion of the ceremonies a Coast Guard cutter in the waters beneath the bridge offered a nineteen-gun salute, other harbor craft sounded their foghorns, and New York City fireboats put on a water-spray show.[3]

There was a brief period in the 1950s when, instead of adding the Lower Level, a bridge across the Hudson at 125th Street was considered. Such a bridge would have routed traffic across Manhattan to the Triborough Bridge, but it would have disrupted city life far more than has the Lower Level of the George Washington Bridge, more than fifty blocks farther uptown. And it would have cost a great deal more.[4]

At one point in the 1920s, Ammann had considered only one barrel cable on each side of the George but had put two to ensure that a second level, if desired, could be added someday. It is remarkable that the Lower Level was added without any additional cabling. Both levels hang from the suspender cables that support the Upper Level and descend from the barrel cables. The Lower Level is simply bolted to the Upper Level by a crosshatch of steel girders.

The most challenging aspect of building the Lower Level was connecting it to a web of approaches and highways on both sides of the river, making certain motorists could reach their desired destination regardless of whether they took the Lower or the Upper Level. Depressed ramps and new tollbooths were constructed in Fort Lee at the approach to the Lower Level. The tunnels under 178th and 179th streets were abandoned, and the twelve-lane Manhattan Expressway was built. It was connected to the Cross Bronx Expressway over the newly constructed Alexander Hamilton Bridge that spanned the Harlem River. In addition, a new bridge headquarters building was erected in Fort Lee and a bus station was built at the eastern end of the bridge, basically to accommodate commuters to and from New York. Also, four apartment towers were built over the Manhattan Expressway to compensate for the apartment buildings taken down to allow its construction. All of these projects proceeded simultaneously with the building of the Lower Level itself, a remarkable feat of coordination.

Although Ammann had long ago left the Port Authority to found his own engineering firm and acted as designer and chief consultant on the Lower Level project, rather than managing its everyday details, his foresight had proven remarkable. First, the Upper Level had to have been hung in 1931 with sufficient clearance between its underside and the bottom of each tower's main arch for another roadway to pass through—a roadway sufficiently elevated above the Hudson to meet Defense Department navigational standards. As it is, the Lower Level is 212 feet above the river at midspan.[5] Also, Ammann, in his original design, had seen to it that steel plates were attached to the Upper Level to which the girders supporting the Lower Level could be bolted.

There were those who felt that the addition of the Lower Level would spoil the bridge's slim good looks. The *New York Times,* at the time of its completion, argued otherwise: "Persons who fear the lovely lines of the George Washington Bridge will be marred by the second deck may be a little relieved to know that Othmar Hermann Ammann, one of this century's master builders of bridges, planned it precisely to carry such a deck. Mr. Ammann at 82 is consulting engineer for the improvement of the structure he completed 30 years ago."[6]

When the Lower Level was added, it was discovered that the extra weight had raised a bump in both roadways. Port Authority engineer Charles Druding, general manager of the Lower Level project, knew that pulling down on adjoining suspender cables would jack up the roadway in the bump areas. But how? Inspecting the cables that needed to be pulled on, Druding discovered that they had handle-like wires attached. Ammann, in the 1920s, had foreseen the bumps and had provided the means of alleviating them.[7]

Another part of the bridge that had to be adjusted when the Lower Level was built was the two 180-ton steel saddles atop each tower, four in all. Under Ammann's supervision, they were each jacked up seven inches to allow the final segment of the Lower Level to be slipped into place. Seventy-five preassembled sections of the Lower Level, each weighing 220 tons, were lifted by cable from barges anchored in the river.

The jacking of the saddles was also necessary to keep the towers vertical. Otherwise, the additional weight of the Lower Deck would have pulled them riverward, that is, bent them toward each other. The jacking compensated by pulling the towers shoreward. Complicating matters further, towers of suspension bridges of substantial length may not be exactly parallel to one another. Their summits are an inch or so farther apart than their bases to allow for the curvature of the earth.

Originally, Ammann had thought that were a Lower Deck ever built, it would be for light rail. However, in 1927, when ground was broken for the George Washington, Henry Ford introduced his Model A automobile, and America's love affair with the car exploded. By 1933, as mentioned earlier, Ammann felt that any new bridge, or addition to a bridge, had to be viewed "primarily as a highway structure, only incidentally accommodating rail traffic."[8] By 1962, virtually all thought of using the Lower Level for trains had been abandoned. Six of the eight lanes were paved for automotive traffic, the two center ones left vacant with the vague thought that they might someday be used for rapid transit tracks. The lanes remain vacant to this day, covered with a thick steel mesh to prevent a vehicle, in a freakish accident, from going over the inside barriers and crashing through to the river. Shortly after the Lower Level opened, a truck did go over a barrier, but the mesh held.

I asked Vicky Kelly, director of Tunnels, Bridges, and Terminals for the Port Authority, why, given the congestion on the bridge, the two vacant lanes on the Lower Level have not been made available for use—which would give the bridge sixteen lanes in all, making it still more busy than any bridge in the world. She told me that it's a question of capacity on the New York side. The off-loading of even more traffic onto the West Side Highway and the Cross Bronx Expressway would be untenable. Nevertheless, she agreed that someday these two lanes might have to be made available for use—but almost certainly for automotive traffic, not mass transit.[9]

By 1962, then, the bridge was exclusively devoted to automotive traffic, and it is likely to remain so. In light of Gustav Lindenthal's railroad bridge dreams, the G.W.B. may be thought of as representative of the triumph of automotive vehicles over mass transit in the twentieth century. Structural engineering professor David Billington writes of "the conversion from an industrialized society dependent upon railroads to one entering the era of large trucks, private automobiles, and suburban decentralization. More than any other structure, perhaps, the George Washington Bridge symbolizes that conversion."[10]

While automotive traffic makes for greater individual freedom, we are more and more discovering its negative effects: pollution, congestion, highway and pedestrian deaths, the loss of community, and the deterioration of mass transit. On average, one bus carries as many passengers as thirty-six automobiles and one train as many passengers as twelve buses. The United States has the worst passenger train system of any nation I know. In the ten years following the opening of the George Washington Bridge in 1931, the Susquehanna Railroad lost over two-thirds of its passengers and would lose even more after the opening of the Lower Level.[11]

There are no walkways on the Lower Level, though this is, perhaps, as it should be. Roofed by the Upper Level and shut in by girders obstructing the view, it is something of a tunnel and would not be a pleasant place to walk or bike. I generally avoid the Lower Level when driving across the bridge. It feels confining and dangerous, only utilitarian and absent any grace. Philip Lopate feels the same way and says he always tries "to edit it out visually to imagine the silvery purity" of the bridge as first constructed.[12] On the Lower Level you are unable to see the towers and the giant barrel cables and the Palisades and the great buildings of Manhattan and the river and the sky. On the Lower Level it is difficult to believe that you are on the same bridge as those enjoying the Upper Level.

The absence of walkways on the Lower Level, while understandable, is symptomatic. By 1962, Robert Moses's automobile-focused plans for New York City were being realized everywhere, and we would see their effect in Ammann's last bridge, the Verrazano-Narrows, where there are no pedestrian or bicycle walkways whatsoever.[13] This is unfortunate. No bridge should be built without walkways. Was Othmar Ammann too much in the thrall of the high-powered Moses when he built the Verrazano that way? In retrospect, we could wish that he had more often considered the social and environmental consequences not only of building a bridge without walkways but of increasingly ignoring mass transit considerations. In this respect he was not a visionary but very much reflected his times.

Similarly, when the huge towers of the Bridge Apartments above the twelve-lane Manhattan Expressway, the road that carries bridge traffic across Manhattan, were built, they were considered an immense novelty and a fashionable address. Although Amman was not involved with them in any way, today we question how anyone could have imagined that homes built above a giant highway might be fit places to live. But Americans had not developed much of an environmental consciousness by 1962. Now we wonder to what extent the people living there are victimized by noxious air rising into their apartments—even though there are huge ventilators underneath the buildings that are supposed to convey elsewhere the exhaust fumes of the three hundred thousand vehicles that daily cross the bridge. Paul Goldberger also has concerns about the apartment towers. "The four towers are identical, poorly detailed slabs, with no concern for light and views. And worst of all, the bridge approach was not fully decked over, so there are immense holes between each tower, bringing the residents a gift of fumes, soot, and noise."[14]

The Bridge Apartments have been dangerous in another way. Ken Philmus says that the greatest crisis he faced as general manager of the G.W.B. was the discovery, in 1989, of a cracked steel girder supporting the buildings. "Replacing it was a *very* delicate operation," he says.[15] A temporary support had to be built, the cracked girder removed, and a new one inserted. Half the incoming Manhattan Expressway was closed for eight or nine days—with two-hour delays in getting across the bridge.

Another perennial problem is the Cross Bronx Expressway, which is where most traffic proceeds after crossing the G.W.B. and the Manhattan Expressway. The Cross Bronx may have been a clever way of keeping bridge through traffic off Manhattan's streets, but, combined with the Bronx River Parkway, which bisects Bronx Park, it had much to do with destroying the Bronx I knew as a boy. Where these highways cross, the Bronx was, in effect, crucified. Divided into four quadrants, with direct communication between them next to impossible, neighborhoods throughout the borough deteriorated.

At the time the Lower Level was inaugurated, the George Washington Bridge Bus Station, designed to relieve congestion by taking commuter buses off the streets of New York, was half a year from completion. Located on one square block between 178th and 179th streets, it opened on January 17, 1963, and is accessed by ramps from the Upper Level of the bridge. Passengers disembarking from buses usually go downstairs and get on the Eighth Avenue Subway, the A train of jazz fame, which runs directly under the bus station. Those accustomed to driving across the George Washington Bridge are usually unaware of the bus station's existence, but it plays a major role in the bridge's overall operation. Handling some forty thousand passengers a day, the bus station is a smaller version of the huge station, the largest in the world, on Eighth Avenue and Forty-first Street in midtown Manhattan.

They are both Port Authority facilities, but the George Washington Bridge Bus Station is an integral part of the bridge. Bridge staff is also responsible for the bus station, and everyone working at the bridge has the bus station as part of his or her title. For example, Bob Durando's full title is general manager, George Washington Bridge and Bus Station; Bob McKee's is physical plant manager, George Washington Bridge and Bus Station.

The bus station was designed by the Italian modernist engineer-architect Pier Luigi Nervi, whose works include the 1960 Olympic Stadium in Rome. Its roof, pairs of tilted reinforced concrete panels resembling butterfly wings, is considered a notable architectural achievement and a fine complement to the bridge. Historian James Morris believes it forms "an integral part of the bridge" and considers it "the neatest and merriest bus station you ever saw." But, writes Paul Goldberger, "the interiors are wretched."[16]

That they are: ill-lit and tacky, with nothing to gladden the eye. The main activity in the station, besides commuters buying a newspaper or a cup of coffee as they rush by, is the gambling at the New York State Off-Track Betting facility that dominates the main concourse. Architecture critic Ada Louise Huxtable refers to the "uniformly dismal enterprises" in the bus station, adding that, whatever its exterior beauty, the interior "exudes an air of abandoned hope."[17]

It is in the lobby of this uninspired bus station interior that the bronze bust of Othmar Amman, unveiled in 1962, is placed—or, shall I say, where it languishes.[18] It sits on a black marble base with a large color photograph of the bridge behind it. Carved on the base are these words:

O. H. Ammann
Designer
George Washington Bridge
1879–1965

I was curious whether people utilizing the bus station know who Ammann was and why his bust is there. When an elderly gentleman emerged from the O.T.B. parlor with the *Daily Racing Form* under his arm and an unlit cigar stub in his mouth, I asked him, "Do you know whose statue this is?"

"What statue?"

"This one over here."

"Oh," he said. He had apparently never noticed the statue before. "Let's see," he said, approaching the statue and fixing his eyes upon Ammann. "Who's he?"

"Othmar Ammann," I said. "He built the George Washington Bridge."

"An Arab built the George Washington Bridge?" he said. "I didn't know that."

"He wasn't an Arab. He was a Swiss immigrant."

"Swiss?!"

"Yes," I said.

"Then how come he has an Arab name?"

On another occasion I interviewed a commuter to see if he knew who Ammann was. This would be someone who probably passes the bust twice a day, five days a week. "Say," I said, to get the attention of the gentleman striding rapidly across the lobby, "do you know whose statue that is?"

"Maybe it's George Washington," he said.

There actually is a bust of George Washington by Frederick von Roth across the lobby from the bust of Othmar Ammann. While the Ammann bust is diminutive but includes his entire upper body—his arms folded on the black marble base, fingers protruding over it—the Washington bust is very large but only comes to midchest. It is a copy of the upper part of the huge equestrian statue of Washington in Morristown, New Jersey, across from the Ford Mansion, Washington's headquarters in the winter of 1779–1780, when his army was quartered down the road in Jockey Hollow.

I pointed to the Washington bust and said, "That's the bust of George Washington."

"Oh," he said, "then maybe the other one's his kid brother. What do I know, man?"

I tried a few more people with similar results. No one knew who that dark bust represented unless, at my suggestion, they actually stopped and read the legend on its pedestal. This was disappointing. I wondered whether the Ammann bust might better be placed on one of the bridge walkways or even in the Administration Building in Fort Lee. In both places it would, I think, be better appreciated.

Still, on one side of the bus station lobby was Ammann, on the other Washington, both heroic figures. It was nice to stand between them and see if I couldn't feel some vibrations, some linkage between them and between them and the great bridge that honors them both. Despite all the noise and bustle and ugliness of the place, their presence did lend it a certain grace.

The bridge during rush hour photographed from the New Jersey side. Courtesy of the Port Authority.

7

Dramas, Dangers, and Disasters

D ESPITE ITS BEAUTY AND GRANDEUR, the George Washington Bridge is occasionally the scene of tragedy. In 2005 two workers fell to their deaths—one in the process of removing scaffolding from the lead abatement and repainting project on the bridge towers, the other from a catwalk inside the New York anchorage.

Motorists have also died in accidents on the bridge. Some have met their fates at the plainly restricted official vehicle turnarounds that my guides used to access the secret places of the bridge. Serious accidents on the bridge have often involved tractor trailers. One tractor trailer went out of control, with its cab ending up extended beyond the walkway on its side and over the water, the passenger side door flung open. The driver, his leg broken, tied himself to the steering wheel to avoid falling out. For fear the truck might break free and descend to the Hudson, no attempt was made to extricate it until the driver had been removed. The only way to get to him was by breaking through the rear window of the cab.

When tractor trailers jackknife on the bridge, they sometimes block all west or eastbound lanes on one level so that, even if there are no fatalities or serious injuries, traffic can become tied up for hours. Some students of mine, who favor the nickname "the Geo" for the George Washington Bridge, tell me that whenever they make a trip that includes crossing it, they take along a marijuana cigarette so they can pass the time in a pleasant manner should they be detained by an accident. I'm not sure how much to credit this story. I suspect they did it once and it has now achieved legendary status in their minds.

When accidents involve motorists and a crime has been committed—such as car theft or drunk driving—or there are serious injuries or a fatality, part of the bridge will be shut down. Usually in major accident situations traffic is diverted to the other level, but there will still be difficulty accessing the accident site: behind it all lanes will often be filled with bumper-to-bumper traffic and, with no shoulder, it will be impossible for emergency vehicles to advance. The trick for the Port Authority, whose equipment is kept behind its Fort Lee offices (in peak traffic hours a wrecker is positioned on the New York side as well), is to get patrol cars, ambulances, tow trucks, and sometimes fire engines to approach from in front of the accident site, where the bridge will likely be entirely clear. Coming from Fort Lee, this is easily accomplished in the westbound lanes, but if the accident is in the eastbound lanes it will usually be necessary to use the other level to cross the bridge, turn around, and return via the affected deck.

The eastbound lanes of the Upper Level once had to be temporarily closed when a truck turned over and spilled a load of watermelons. Another time it was fourteen thousand pounds of frozen chicken parts. Another time it was Bolivian beer. Another time it was goats spilling out of a truck and running across the bridge. Yet another time it was a cargo of horse manure; while bridge employees frantically shoveled, motorists, who were detained behind the accident anyway, helped themselves to quantities of free fertilizer for their gardens. Occasionally, traffic is stopped for some hours on the Upper Level not by an accident but by high winds.

Cars that break down or are abandoned on the bridge, of course, have to be towed off. Sometimes an abandoned car suggests a suicide, but on other occasions there is no ready explanation. Eventually, it is discovered that someone, apparently disgusted with a car's performance, simply walked away from it on, of all places, the George Washington Bridge. One Port Authority patrolman told me he came upon a car stopped on the bridge and holding up traffic. Inquiring what the problem was, he was asked, with an urgent tone, "Where's the bathroom?"

Then there are motorists—usually with a fear of heights and/or bridges—who have a panic attack and simply halt their cars at midbridge. A Port Authority patrol car is dispatched with two officers, one to drive the frightened motorist's car across. Years ago, Port Authority patrolmen assisted a woman afraid of heights who panicked, stopped on the bridge, and sat there shaking. An officer got into her car and behind the wheel. But, reported the then chief of bridge security, "the woman got so frightened continuing across the bridge, even with the policeman driving, that she was almost in the officer's lap and thrashing about with fear as he tried to drive. Afterwards, people phoned to say that a woman was kidnapped and molested in a car by a policeman on the bridge."[1]

A vehicle fire or hazardous material spill is a particularly difficult situation for bridge management. In 1980, for the first time in the almost half century since the bridge opened, both levels were entirely closed when a leaking valve on a tanker carrying nine thousand gallons of propane gas generated fears of an explosion and fire engulfing a large portion of the bridge. Luckily, someone on the bridge maintenance staff found a cork with which he was able to temporarily plug the leak.[2]

The most famous accident on the George Washington took place on Christmas Day 1965, when a plane crash-landed on the Upper Level. A nineteen-year-old pilot from the Bronx, Philip Ippolito, was out for a pleasure ride with a friend in a small plane he had rented at the Ramapo Valley Airport in Spring Valley, New York. They flew down the Hudson, developing what they thought was engine trouble just off midtown Manhattan. Ippolito turned the plane around, thinking he might be able to make it back to the airport. But the engine was now sputtering. He thought the safest thing was to ditch in the freezing Hudson but was persuaded otherwise when his passenger, Joseph F. Brennan Jr., said he couldn't swim. Ippolito also realized that the Aeronca Champion was a fixed landing gear airplane. Without retractable landing gear, there was little chance he could set the plane's belly down on the Hudson without the wheels first catching in the water and the plane flipping over.

Earlier, in flying over the George Washington Bridge, he had noticed that traffic was light, as it usually is on a Sunday. With his engine now close to failing altogether, he glided toward the bridge and managed a long sweeping curve over the lowest point of the south barrel cables. He even avoided the concrete divider between the four eastbound and four westbound lanes. His plane, with a thirty-four-foot wingspan, set down between widely spaced westbound cars and trucks. However, it came in too fast behind a truck driven by Woodrow F. Leone, who said: "I was driving along about 40, and I just happened to glance in my side

The plane crash-landed on the bridge by pilot Philip Ippolito, Christmas Day 1965. Courtesy of the Port Authority.

view mirror and saw this plane coming up on me. . . . I didn't know what to think or do."

The plane's wing clipped the truck, causing almost no damage to it, but the plane was pretty well demolished when it spun out of control and then smacked into the concrete divider. There was no fire because the plane's problem, as it turned out, was that it was out of fuel; its gas cap was missing. Ippolito and Brennan were able to disembark without assistance and were taken to the hospital. Ippolito had bruises over much of his body; Brennan had a deep cut in his chin, which required a dozen stitches, and lost a front tooth. Both men were released from the hospital two days later.[3]

HAD MICHAEL TEEL BEEN ON DUTY on Christmas Day 1965, he might have been involved in documenting Ippolito's and Brennan's adventure. Teel is a big, friendly Port Authority patrolman with a walrus-like mustache. He's the son of John Teel, who spent much of his career as an electrician on the bridge, and the father of Rutgers University's 2006–2008 starting quarterback, Mike Teel. Michael Teel's special responsibility is investigating accidents at Port Authority facilities. For example, he investigated the crash on February 5, 2005, of an improperly loaded plane at Teterboro Airport that, unable to lift off, burst through the airport's perimeter fence, skidded across all six lanes of Route 46—damaging two cars along the way—and then smashed into a warehouse, which sent a shower of bricks down on it. There were thirteen injuries but, luckily, no fatalities.[4]

At 3:00 A.M. on September 11, 2001, Teel was investigating an accident on the George Washington Bridge involving two tractor trailers westbound on the Upper Level. One of the drivers had a severed leg and had to be immediately evacuated. By 5:00 A.M. the trucks had been removed to an impoundment yard in Ridgefield Park, New Jersey, where Teel continued his work, assessing the damage to the two trucks. He was still there, preparing to go home to catch some rest, when the first plane hit the World Trade Center. Teel drove to G.W.B. headquarters in Fort Lee. When several New Jersey fire trucks arrived, he escorted them across the bridge and down to the World Trade Center site. Teel would remain there, digging, for the better part of the next forty-eight hours.[5]

The Port Authority built and managed the World Trade Center and occupied nineteen floors in Tower I, where two thousand of their seven thousand employees had their offices. Talking to Michael Teel about

9/11, as when talking about that subject to anyone who is with the Port Authority, the conversation can go just so far. Midway, their eyes tear up and they can't go on. Of the eighty-four Port Authority employees who lost their lives that day, nearly half were Teel's fellow policemen.

Steve Napolitano, now assistant director of the Tunnels, Bridges, and Terminals Division of the Port Authority, was general manager of the George Washington Bridge on 9/11. Napolitano grew up in Fort Lee, New Jersey, so when he got the job as manager of the bridge "it was like going home. And my kids were so proud that this was now 'Dad's bridge.'" Napolitano, like Bob Durando, was general manager of the Holland Tunnel prior to his assignment to the G.W.B. "It was like going from the minors to the big leagues" is the way he describes his job change. And now that he is in a supervisory position at Port Authority headquarters, he misses "being in the action at the bridge. Everything goes across that bridge: wide loads that have to be escorted—such as mobile homes that take up two lanes; circus animals; heads of state with motorcycle escorts. When that bridge is humming it's a symphony of coordination."

On September 11, 2001, the bridge stopped humming. Napolitano faced a situation without precedent. "When the planes hit I didn't know what to do. I had no guidance from headquarters because there *was* no headquarters; it had been in the World Trade Center. I couldn't very well call the person in the position I'm in now for advice. I'm getting my information from television, and I'm wondering whether they're going to hit the G.W.B. next. We cleared off all traffic already on the bridge heading east, though we let traffic coming out of the city run for a while. Traffic heading toward the bridge in New Jersey had to be turned around. Then we locked down the bridge, closing all lanes on both levels except for emergency vehicles—police, firemen, E.M.S. Everyone wanted to go down to the World Trade Center but, except for a few patrolmen who were dispatched down there, Bruce Reynolds and the others, we had to stay at the bridge. We were constantly opening a couple of lanes to get emergency personnel through and then buttoning them up again. We were a staging area for men and materials going to the W.T.C. Nobody left the G.W.B. Administration Building to go home for three days."[6]

Just after the bridge was closed, a small plane landed at Teterboro carrying a heart meant for Doug "Mackey" Goodwin, who once played football for the Buffalo Bills and was being prepared for immediate surgery at Columbia Presbyterian Hospital just across the bridge in Washington Heights. The plane had taken off from Boston's Logan

Airport immediately behind the two jets en route to attacking the World Trade Center. The pilot of the small plane could see them and, knowing via radio that they were supposedly bound elsewhere, wondered why they were heading toward New York City. At Teterboro, the heart was placed in an ambulance, but by the time it arrived at the George Washington, the bridge had been closed down. "One driver was going to get out and walk it across the bridge," said Goodwin, but this proved unnecessary when bridge staff got wind of what was going on and shepherded the ambulance across.[7]

"We also ran shuttles for people who arrived at the bridge on foot and needed to get home," Steve Napolitano says. "Meanwhile, family of Port Authority personnel are calling me because there's no one to call at headquarters. I'm crying, but I don't want them to know; I wanted to sound relaxed and like I knew what I was doing, even if I didn't. And, meanwhile, these F-14 fighter jets are roaring up and down the Hudson River like it's World War III. It was surreal."

The George Washington slowly returned to a relatively normal state over the next few days (although current general manager Bob Durando says, "We've never really returned to 'normal' and probably never should"), with discussions already under way on ways to radically increase the number of cameras trained on the bridge and to reinforce certain areas that could easily be damaged by a bomb blast. Private security services were hired and stationed in booths along the walkways where the barrel cables pass through on their way to the anchorages and on both sides of the two towers, as well as at the base of the towers. These areas were also encapsulated by high steel fences topped with barbed wire. One measure immediately instituted and still in effect confined the thirty thousand to forty thousand large commercial vehicles using the bridge each day to the Upper Level. "This is because of the tunnel effect," Napolitano says. "If a terrorist truck blew up on the Upper Deck, most of the force of the explosion would dissipate into the air. But if it blew up between decks, the concentrated explosion would do much more damage." Trucks that mistakenly get into bridge approaches accessing the Lower Deck are routinely stopped, searched by Port Authority patrolmen, and sometimes issued summonses before being turned away. Particular attention is paid to rental trucks because of their connection with terrorist incidents, especially the 1993 bombing of the World Trade Center and the 1995 bombing of the Alfred P. Murrah Federal Building in Oklahoma City. However, vans, perhaps because of uncertainty as to whether they are "trucks" or not, occasionally get through these barriers, leading to 911 calls to the police and letters to the editor from worried Lower Level motorists who observe them crossing the bridge.[8]

Napolitano says that the greatest problem of his staff in the aftermath of 9/11 was psychological. "We had all lost friends. I can't remember how many funerals I went to."

Ken Philmus, former general manger of the George Washington and director of Tunnels, Bridges, and Terminals on 9/11, remembers exactly how many funerals he attended: thirty-five. He says, "If I ever hear one more bagpipe I'll scream." Luckily, he was in Boston at a meeting on 9/11 rather than in his office on the sixty-fourth floor of Tower I. He visited the homes of some of the eleven murdered staff members who worked under his direction. One of them, Patrick Hoey, was famous at the Port Authority for always saying, "We must leave these facilities better than we received them." In Hoey's home, a three-by-seven-foot photograph of the George Washington Bridge hung over the living room sofa. Philmus sat down and cried.[9] I have never been in anyone's office at the George Washington Bridge or at Port Authority headquarters in Manhattan who did not have prominently displayed pictures of friends and colleagues lost on 9/11.

In the aftermath of 9/11, the G.W.B. staff was challenged by a situation without precedent. To build not only their own morale but that of the general public, the sixty-by-ninety-foot American flag was deployed from the New Jersey tower. Napolitano and his staff also resurrected from the basement of bridge headquarters a retired flag. In spare time and when off duty, they repaired this flag and, when it was in decent shape, took it to downtown Manhattan and stretched it across the façade of a damaged public school near the World Trade Center site. "That made everyone feel a bit better," Napolitano says. "It was therapy," says Jerry Del Tufo, then physical plant manager at the bridge. Del Tufo, like many present and past staff at the bridge, has a photograph of the flag stretched across that school hanging on his office wall.[10]

A SECURITY CONCERN LONG PREDATING 9/11 that continues today is suicide prevention. The G.W.B. averages slightly more than one "successful" suicide a month and several attempts. When I mention these figures, people are startled. "How come we never hear about these suicides?" they ask. They don't because the Port Authority has a conscious policy of keeping silent about suicides as best it can so as not to inspire copycat "jumpers," as bridge officials call them.

The managers of the Golden Gate Bridge at the other end of America call them jumpers too, but they make no effort to suppress news of suicides. Quite the contrary. Authorities in San Francisco seem to feel obligated to cooperate with the media in reporting suicides on the Golden Gate. In the 1970s, two San Francisco newspapers, the *Chronicle* and the *Examiner,* featured a countdown to the five hundredth recorded jumper. There were actually fourteen aspirants to the title, including one man with the number 500 pinned to his shirt. Eventually a young man eluded bridge officials and claimed the "honor." In 1995, the bridge was approaching one thousand recorded jumpers, and the media was covering this new landmark as if it were a major sporting event. A disc jockey was known to have offered a case of Snapple to the family of the victim.[11] Some years later, a filmmaker was permitted to make a documentary chronicling jumper deaths from the Golden Gate during one year.[12]

An aside, irresistible in its irony: In 1977, a minister held a rally of six hundred of his flock at the bridge supporting the building of a suicide barrier arching over the walkway. He claimed that while the Golden Gate was a symbol of "technological genius," it was also a symbol of "social failure." Eighteen months later, in far-off Guyana, that same minister, Jim Jones, presided over the deaths of 912 of his followers from cyanide-laced Kool-Aid.[13]

The Golden Gate has twice as many suicides as the George Washington, or about two dozen per year. A friend of mine, Jon Robertson, has lived much of his life either in California or in the Greater New York area. When I told him of this numerical disparity, he responded, his tongue only partially in his cheek, "That's easy to explain. Californians are laid-back; they have such an Eden-like vision of life that when having a bad day they jump off the Golden Gate. People in New York and New Jersey know that life can be tough and ugly, so when things aren't going well they figure, 'That's just the way it is,' and it doesn't occur to them to go jump off the George Washington Bridge."

I don't know about the accuracy of Robertson's comment on East and West Coast culture, but it made me think of two things. First, a joke: "How many Californians does it take to change a lightbulb? A dozen. One to change the lightbulb, eleven to experience it." Second, it made me think of that T-shirt popular in my part of the country with the slogan NEW JERSEY: ONLY THE TOUGH SURVIVE.[14] That both the gritty music of Bruce Springsteen and *The Sopranos* are New Jersey products suggests that there might be some wisdom in that T-shirt. Key words in New Jersey (and in New York City as well) are "street smarts," "attitude," and "chutzpah." A more hardheaded approach to life may account for a suicide rate lower on the G.W.B. than on the Golden Gate. It is possible that the rate on the G.W.B. would be even lower were it not for what has come to be called "Suicide Tourism"—which refers to unfortunates from elsewhere who travel to New Jersey or New York and out onto the bridge, choosing to end their lives in a place with a certain glamour.[15] No doubt such "tourism" affects the numbers of suicides on the Golden Gate as well.

But, again, with a certain difference. For some reason, although the bridges are nearly the same height, over the years twenty-six people have survived leaps from the Golden Gate, and only two have survived jumps from the George Washington. Jokes Jon Robertson, "That's the laid-back part of Californians I was telling you about. They're so relaxed, they bounce."[16]

One of the two George Washington Bridge survivors was a man who drove onto the bridge with his mother, stopped the car, and leaped over the railing. Though he broke his back, he managed to make it to shore. The other was a Chinese American woman who, pulled from the water, was discovered to have broken virtually every bone in her body. She spent a year in the hospital being slowly knit back together. Released, she immediately made her way back to the George Washington and jumped again. This time she was "successful."

An Edgewater, New Jersey, man, Paul Tierney, bet a friend five hundred dollars in 1971 that he could jump from the bridge and survive. Edgewater is a small town on the banks of the Hudson just south of the bridge. The George Washington is constantly in sight, and daily exposure to the bridge may, in part, have accounted for Tierney's bravado. In any case, technically he won the bet. He "survived," but died three days later of internal injuries.[17]

The possibility of suicide on the bridge is never far from the minds of G.W.B. officials. They are ever on the alert and manage to stop two or three potential suicides for every one who goes over the side. They have so far rejected enclosing the walkways with some sort of wire mesh because it would make the bridge ugly and the journey over it on foot or by bicycle considerably less desirable. Also, as a Port Authority patrolman who wished to remain anonymous said to me, "If they can't jump here, they'll jump somewhere else. Better they hit the water. If they jump from a building they might kill someone below. Here they just kill themselves."

In the lobby of bridge headquarters, just outside the Communications Center, signs are sometimes posted with pictures of missing persons who may have jumped off the bridge. One, dated May 30, 2006, gave the person's name and these ominous words: "His last known location was the George Washington Bridge, at approximately 4:30 A.M." Signs are also posted in the lobby from time to time naming the Employee of the Month, often someone who helped avert a suicide.

There was hardly a present or past G.W.B. staff person I interviewed who didn't have his or her own tale of witnessing a suicide or participating in averting one. While Ken Philmus was general manager, a man threatening to jump said he would reconsider if he were delivered into the care of a doctor. Philmus, who had gone out onto the bridge with other staff trying to avert a tragedy, happened to have a white shirt and tie on. He played the doctor role, and a life was saved.[18]

Other staffers told me about "the Tuxedo Jumper," who has appeared on the bridge from time to time in a tuxedo and climbed up into a tower, then been talked down. He is likely to have done it for the last time; post 9/11, the towers are so enclosed by fencing that accessing them would be near impossible.

One man was on the point of jumping when a Port Authority patrolman drew his gun and said, "Stop or I'll shoot." He stopped.

A book featuring the story of a man who climbed to the top of one of the G.W.B. towers planning to kill himself but changed his mind is titled *Go Ahead, Jump!*[19]

Shock jock Howard Stern had a young Bronx man call into his radio show on a cell phone from midspan on the north walkway of the G.W.B. at 8:10 the morning of December 7, 1994. Stern found him "so annoying . . . I was going to tell him to jump." Then Stern realized that was exactly what the man had in mind. Motorists driving west who were listening to Stern's program stopped their cars on the bridge and tried to talk the man out of jumping. A few borrowed his phone to chat with Stern. Luckily, a Port Authority policeman back at bridge headquarters in Fort Lee was listening to the radio and immediately set forth for the spot with several colleagues. At one point the man's connection failed, and Stern said, "I guess he jumped." But the man came back on in a moment, saying, "My battery is running low and so am I." By this time the police had arrived and successfully took the man into custody. They used his phone to tell Stern that all was well and that they were big fans of his.[20]

Probably the most dramatic suicide attempt in the George Washington Bridge's history took place on June 1, 2007. A man managed to get up on the barrel cables at their midspan low point, where they are only fifteen feet above the sidewalk. He apparently mounted the walkway barrier and then shimmied up a light stanchion, since removed. He was on barrel cable C, the inside cable on the north side, ascending it toward the New Jersey tower. When he was spotted, at 7:00 A.M., all traffic was halted on the Upper Level. Those already on it, including bikers and pedestrians, were not allowed to proceed. If the man had jumped, he could easily have killed someone below. Traffic on both sides of the bridge was backed up for miles, and since trucks are not allowed

The barrel cables at their lowest point, where the man who considered suicide on June 1, 2007, mounted and began his journey up toward the New Jersey tower. Courtesy of the Port Authority.

on the Lower Level they had to pull over and await the end of the crisis. Adding to the problem: this was rush hour. The only things moving were the news helicopters noisily swarming about the bridge.

The police did not know what this individual had in mind, suicide or terrorism. It didn't help that, through binoculars, he could be seen to be carrying a box cutter like the ones used on 9/11. Bridge staffers got the police into harnesses, then took one squad of them up to the north saddle room in the elevators so they could access the cable from above. Another squad was helped to mount the cable below, where the man had gotten on. By this time the man was up near the top of the cable, some 550 feet in the air. On Cable D, the outside cable on the north side, a single police officer skilled in hostage and suicide negotiations descended to a point opposite the man and kept talking to him as the police closed in from both sides. However, now the man began threatening the police with the box cutter, swinging it wildly. When they backed off he sat on the cable and slashed at his own wrists and arms, bleeding profusely. In ensuing days, macabre humor among G.W.B. staff included: "It was bad enough that guy went up there, but did he also have to bleed all over the new paint job?"

After an hour or so of negotiations, the man dropped the box cutter, and the police quickly moved in. They put harnesses on the man and walked him up to the top of the tower so they could access the elevators, bring him down, and get him to a hospital. Traffic across the Upper Level resumed at 9:20 A.M. Tens of thousands of people were late for work that day.

A week or so later this same man, released from the hospital, showed up twice at the Communications Center in the lobby of the G.W.B. Administration Building in Fort Lee. The second time he wrote a note thanking the police "for saving my life."

The bridge at night. Courtesy of the Port Authority.

The George Washington Bridge in Literature

BRIDGES HAVE A FIGURATIVE as well as a literal utility. For some writers, they serve as metaphors for what brings people together and, also, for what divides them. For others, they are emblematic of the collision between nature and the human-built environment. For others still, they provide a romantic or dramatic backdrop for events. A random sample comes immediately to mind: James Michener's *The Bridges at Toko-Ri*; Pierre Boulle's *The Bridge over the River Kwai*; Ernest Hemingway's *For Whom the Bell Tolls*; Cornelius Ryan's *A Bridge Too Far*; Robert James Waller's *The Bridges of Madison County*; Henry Wadsworth Longfellow's fine poem "The Bridge"; and, of course, Hart Crane's series of poems inspired by the Brooklyn Bridge, also titled *The Bridge*. I'll discuss here only a few representative works in which the George Washington Bridge is central to the story or, at least, the focus of an important scene.

Adult Fiction

Permit me to violate this promise immediately by discussing minor mentions in two short stories too charming to ignore. A friend, Nami Mun, talks about her Korean father's naturalization, when he was asked by a stern INS agent a series of basic American history questions, including "Who was the first president of the United States?"

"George Washington Bridge," he answered proudly. The INS agent laughed and gave him a pass on that question.[1]

Immigrants are proverbially more fervent in their Americanism than those of us born here. In an Edgar Rosenberg short story in which a Jewish refugee family from Nazi Germany has settled in Washington Heights, the protagonist's mother will tolerate nothing but praise for the George Washington Bridge and its Americanness. At one point her husband needles her by saying, " 'The George Washington Bridge was built by a Swiss,' but she turned a deaf ear to such foul-mouthed language."[2]

Now on to major works: first, two novels that present the bridge as a grimly appropriate place for a suicide.

In James Baldwin's *Another Country*, Rufus, a black jazz musician, despairs not only about his life but about his country. Like Baldwin himself, who left America because he found its racism intolerable, Rufus ultimately seeks a way out:

> Suddenly he knew that he was never going home any more.... *You took the best. So why not take the rest?* He got off at the station named for the bridge built to honor the father of his country.... Then he stood on the bridge, looking over, looking down.... There were muted lights on the Jersey shore. He thought, You bastard, you motherfucking bastard. Ain't I your baby too? ...
> He was black and the water was black.
> He lifted himself by his hands on the rail, lifted himself as high as he could and leaned far out. The wind tore at him ... and then the wind took him.... He felt a shoe fly off behind him ... *All right you ... bastard, I'm coming to you.*[3]

This is one of the most powerful scenes in all of Baldwin's work and equally powerful as an indictment of America. The fact that Rufus—who felt he could never be a true child of his country because of his race—decides to kill himself on the bridge named for the father of our country should resonate painfully for all of us.

In Howard Fast's novel *Redemption* the main action essentially begins with the chapter "The Woman on the Bridge." In it the protagonist, a seventy-eight-year-old retired professor and lonely widower, is driving back from New Jersey to Manhattan across the G.W.B. at 3:30 in the morning when he spots a woman in her forties standing at the rail of the south pedestrian walkway.

Stopped about a dozen feet from her, I said, "I wouldn't if I were you. It might not kill you at all, and that would leave you with months of agony in the hospital—worse than whatever pain you're in now."

Of course, it would have killed her, but that was all I could invent at the moment. She turned to face me. . . . She asked softly, "How did you know?"

"Because I've opened that door a hundred times."

"What door?"

"The door you are looking at."

Thus begins a July-December relationship that will carry on through the novel, with both characters achieving redemption through their growing love for each other.[4]

Anne Richardson Roiphe's *Up the Sandbox* is an early feminist novel that is a near dramatization of Betty Friedan's classic *The Feminine Mystique*. Its protagonist, a Manhattan housewife with children, imagines other lives for herself in alternate chapters—the "Out-of-Week" chapters that follow the "In-Week" chapters. In Out-of-Week One she is the only white member of a radical group whose name forms the acronym PROWL. PROWL plans to blow up the George Washington Bridge. She wishes to perform a task "that would result in . . . the destruction of an engineering marvel, the undoing of a technological wonder." She wants to see millions of cars, "now idle in garages, choke on their own oils and rust." She and her confederates are placing charges when a prospective suicide moves out onto the bridge. Rejecting her qualms about blowing up the bridge just then, the leader of PROWL, her lover, insists, "You can't murder a suicide"—a corollary of the real-life story of the policeman who foiled a suicide by yelling, "Stop or I'll shoot."

When the group begins setting off the charges, the suicide, now afraid for his life, tries in vain to save himself. But "one of the towers broke in three places . . . a cable broke loose from its top mooring and swung down over the bridge like a huge octopus tentacle reaching into the darkness for a victim." Slowly the bridge collapses into the Hudson River. It is a powerful and frightening scene, but, of course, it is fantasy. Part of the fantasy is that there are absolutely no vehicles whatsoever on the bridge when it is destroyed—something that could never happen on the busy George. In the next chapter, In-Week Two, the protagonist is back with her family going about her normal pursuits. *Up the Sandbox,* published in 1970, reminds us that there was a time before 9/11 when terrorist acts could be played almost as comedy.[5]

Up the Sandbox was made into a movie with Barbra Streisand playing the lead role.[6] The movie poster showed Streisand tied to a giant baby bottle. But in the movie, PROWL blows up the Statue of Liberty instead of the George Washington Bridge—for logistical and economic reasons, I suspect. The scene could be more easily created with an establishing shot of the statue and a set representing a portion of its dark interior, no doubt created of wood and canvas on a studio soundstage. It would have been much more difficult and costly to create a believable George Washington Bridge set of even modest proportions.

A Bridge to Love, by Nancy Herkness, might appear to have feminist implications because its female protagonist is an engineer, but the novel is actually a chick lit romance in the Berkley Sensations series, with unforgivably cute lines such as "Randall quirked an eyebrow." Nevertheless, the George Washington Bridge is more central to this novel than to any other I've found. Herkness, a resident of Glen Ridge, New Jersey, obviously did some research on the nearby bridge.

On the cover of the book, Kate Chilton's dreamy face is superimposed over a photograph with the little red lighthouse in the foreground and the G.W.B. looming overhead. Kate loves the George Washington Bridge, and it proves to be a pathway to an initially problematical love—thus the double entendre of the title.

Following standard romance formula, there are two main male figures: one a fair-haired nice guy the female protagonist wishes she was attracted to but feels no passion for; the other a dark, mysterious, sexy but dangerous, and seemingly unknowable man who is finally revealed as Mr. Right when, with her irresistible allure, the protagonist tames if not domesticates him. He falls in love with her and, through her, with the George Washington Bridge.

Kate is newly widowed with two young boys. Now she needs a job, and she lands one designing a bridge, for her the ultimate professional prize. Happily, she muses that she can "still think like an engineer" and that the forthcoming project will be like "building the George Washington Bridge itself." For years Kate has treasured blueprints of the George Washington, and now she takes them out and traces "its soaring piers and curving cables with familiar affection and admiration."

Othmar Ammann is her "all-time hero." (You have to wonder what the modest and shy Ammann would have thought about that.)

On her way home to New Jersey one evening with her new love, Randall Johnson, Kate says, "I love this route home. It's got a whole symphony of bridges along it . . . and it all crescendos to the big guy, the George Washington Bridge. That's my favorite."

"I've never known anyone who had a favorite bridge," Randall says.

"You don't know many engineers then," Kate replies. "One of our best Sunday afternoon outings with the boys was walking across the George Washington Bridge. David [her deceased husband] loved the simple, functional lines of it. The boys loved being two hundred feet in the air. I loved everything about it, but especially the fact that mankind could conceive of and create such a grand structure for such a practical purpose."

Randall responds, "I see that I'll have to reexamine my view of bridges. Maybe I could join one of those Sunday afternoon outings."

But before wedding bells can ring, Kate and Randall are hunted down by killers tailing them on the Upper Level. They abandon their car and run along the walkway. Kate knows the bridge so well she finds a hiding place for them on the underside of the Upper Level's steel support girders, the ones Ammann used to stiffen his slim roadway. There she "literally held her breath and thanked her lucky stars that the Port Authority budget didn't allow for illuminating the towers except on holidays." In the requisite scene where the heroine, however liberated, must be saved by the hero, Randall, with rippling muscles, holds Kate dangling over the river with one arm while supporting both of them by clinging to a girder with the other. Kate's bodice isn't ripped, but her pantyhose is in pretty bad shape.

Finally, the Port Authority police arrive, the killers flee, and the enamored pair return to their car to discover that, in the emergency, all traffic in the westbound lanes had been halted for them. As Randall starts the car, Kate says, "Go slowly, I've never been the only car on the bridge. . . . I want to enjoy the view."

"After what you've been through you want to look at a bridge?" Randall responds.

"It took care of us, didn't it?" she asks.

"I guess it did." We know that Randall's conversion to loving Kate— and the George Washington Bridge as well—is complete when he exclaims, "Look at the size of those cables."[7]

If my more sentimental readers' eyes are now moist, the many hard-boiled novels that use the G.W.B. as a noir locale should dry them quick. One of them, Alice Hoffman's *Property Of,* has a female protagonist who, unlike Kate Chilton, is one tough cookie. In a car riding westward on the Upper Level, she tells the driver, for whom she hankers, to pull over. She explains, "I want to fuck you, but not in New Jersey." At this point the couple proceed to, well, couple. I'll ignore the insult to New Jersey but point out that no one could pull over on the G.W.B. without a patrol car, lights flashing, arriving in a minute or two.

Nevertheless, I've been told that sex on the George Washington Bridge is a common female fantasy. I have no idea if this is correct but discovered years ago that the New Jersey Turnpike is a similarly favored locale in the fantasy lives of some women.[8]

Donald Westlake, under the pseudonym of Richard Stark, wrote another tough story involving the bridge, *The Hunter,* a tale of revenge. Parker, the protagonist, has been double-crossed by his partner, shot by his wife, and left for dead in a burning building. The novel begins on the New Jersey side of the bridge with a tone more than a little reminiscent of Mickey Spillane's unremitting, often misogynistic, malice:

> When a fresh-faced guy in a Chevy offered him a lift, Parker told him to go to hell. The guy said, "Screw you, buddy," yanked his Chevy back into the stream of traffic, and roared on down to the tollbooths. Parker spat in the right-hand lane, lit his last cigarette, and walked across the George Washington Bridge.
>
> ... [On the other side there were] lanes and lanes of nobody going to Jersey. Underneath, the same thing.
>
> Out in the middle, the bridge trembled and swayed in the wind.... He felt it shivering under his feet, and he got mad. He threw the used-up butt at the ocean, spat on a passing hubcap, and strode on.
>
> Office women in passing cars looked at him and felt vibrations above their nylons. He was big and shaggy, with flat square shoulders.... His face was a chipped chunk of concrete, with eyes of flawed onyx. His mouth was a quick stroke, bloodless.

Parker is the classic antihero, with lots of free-floating hostility and, of course, fulfilling male fantasies, all the "dames" in the novel are crazy about him on sight.

But to clear up a few facts: There isn't a spot at the approaches to the tollbooths where any kind of hero, anti or otherwise, can be offered a ride; only a world-class spitter could possibly hit a rapidly moving hubcap; and the Hudson, at the point where Parker throws his cigarette into it, is a tidal estuary, not the ocean. Also, there are those of us who take issue with the suggestion that anyone heading for New Jersey is a "nobody." However, none of this stopped Hollywood from twice making films inspired by *The Hunter: Point Blank* (1967), starring Lee Marvin, and *Payback* (1999), starring Mel Gibson.[9]

Another dark book in which the George Washington Bridge figures importantly is Adrian McKinty's *Dead I Well May Be*. Full of gangsters, homeless people, hard drugs, and general seaminess, much of the novel takes place on the Upper West Side of Manhattan, often in the shadow of the George Washington Bridge. For its protagonist, Michael, the bridge is a looming though never noble or attractive presence throughout the book: "It was foggy and dense and rain came and changed the landscape to a better one, erasing the gray Hudson and New Jersey and all but the closest towers [there are, of course, only two towers in all] of the suspension bridge. With the fog and the ghost bridge, you could be anywhere." Michael seems to like it that way because later he says, "It was dark and the lights were on over New Jersey and the George Washington Bridge. The fog was gone and I thought that was a pity."

At one point Michael is dropped off on the New Jersey side of the bridge when "it was raining and cold and night.... I walked over the GWB in the drizzly dark. There's no toll for pedestrians, thank Christ, for I had only a dollar and fifty-seven cents ... and with that I took the A train to 125th St."

On another occasion he walks across the bridge to the New Jersey side and enters the woods of Palisades Interstate Park, following a road down to the undercliff. He thinks, "Jesus, half the population of New Jersey is going over the bridge above us, but down here it's all quiet, peaceful, no witnesses at all." The "no witnesses" hints that Michael is not there to enjoy nature. He's being followed by two goons, and soon the brief pastoral scene is shattered when Michael kills them both and dumps their bodies in the woods below the bridge. Then he takes their car and drives back across the bridge to execute the man who sent them.[10]

In a different vein entirely, Philip Seplow's short story "Andy and the Tomato," concerns a tomato farmer, Andy Harlin, who lives in Tenafly,

New Jersey, not far from the bridge. His wife has left him because of his obesity. When they married he weighed 168 pounds; now he weighs 300. She had urged him, to no avail, to eat his own tomatoes instead of the Hostess Twinkies he favors.

One day, in his kitchen, he hears a voice and realizes it is coming from a large tomato. The tomato increases exponentially in size, rolls outside into his yard, and soon is the size of an elephant. Touching the tomato, Andy is swallowed up by it. Now the tomato starts rolling toward the George Washington Bridge, followed by the police and by news helicopters. It is a major story, on all the channels. The tomato rolls across the G.W.B. and eventually into Central Park. Meanwhile, inside, Andy is running laps, his only sustenance a bit of soft tomato from time to time. His estranged wife, learning of his plight, arrives on the scene and, on touching the tomato, is also swallowed up by it. She discovers Andy inside, now back to 168 pounds, and the two emerge from the tomato reunited.

I'm not sure what to make of this playful story, whether it is simply a commentary on a nation obsessed with diets but plagued by obesity or has some deeper meaning. In any case, the picture of a giant tomato rolling across the George Washington Bridge is memorable. Then too, I feel some kinship with Andy himself: "Andy Harlin always thought that the George Washington Bridge was the most magnificent structure ever built across water and grew frustrated when listening to Northern Californians talk about the Golden Gate Bridge." Andy's vision is vindicated. With all the publicity the George Washington gets because of the giant tomato racing across it and the romantic, very public conclusion to Andy and his wife's story, "The George . . . would once again stake its claim as the greatest bridge in the world."[11]

Poetry

Not many have seen the naked steel of the durably designed George Washington Bridge as the stuff of poetry. However, engineer David Steinman, who was also a poet, once wrote that "a bridge is a poem stretching across a river."[12] And the G.W.B. itself has inspired several poets. At the bridge's inauguration, Louis Hoebel, mayor of Fort Lee, read a long poem by a Fort Lee resident, the Reverend Vincent Burns, titled with one of the names considered for the George.

The Rainbow Bridge

The spirit of George Washington is marching in the van
Of the countless human army that will cross this glorious span
In the next one hundred centuries of this marvelous age of
      man. . . .

The spirit of George Washington has come back to lead the way,
He is marching with his people to another, modern fray
Where the poor and weak are praying for a new and brighter
      day. . . .

This wonderful achievement is a bright prophetic gleam
Of the world that man will enter when he builds the social scheme
As nobly and as wisely as he spanned this mighty stream.

When man conquers unemployment as he conquers gravity,
When he scales the cliffs of hunger with his comrade Industry,
When he builds a bridge of hope above the deeps of poverty. . . .

O, spirit of George Washington! your people hear the call,
As wove these shining cables, as we reared these towers tall
We will build a mighty nation as a freedom home for all.[13]

Clearly this poem—though overly heroic and sentimental to contemporary tastes; I have spared the reader half of it—expresses the spirit of its times, with the Depression weighing on America. The bridge and George Washington himself here are emblematic of the progress and decency of which humankind is capable.

In chapter 4, I mentioned a poem by William Meredith called "The Cemetery Bridge," inspired by the apocryphal story that a man or some men were entombed in the wet concrete of the New York anchorage. Here is the poem:

Well, as you all should know, there's a dead man
in the George Washington Bridge.
How he got there, they was digging and drilling
those real deep holes for the pillows

of the George Washington Bridge.
While they was digging and drilling, a man fell in.
Of course he was dead, but we will never know for sure.
So they pay his family millions of dollars
So they won't have to dig him up and start all over again.
Please spread this story around.[14]

Diane Wakoksi published a book of twenty-three poems titled *The George Washington Poems,* and in one of them, "George Washington, Man and Monument," the poet, as critic Alicia Ostriker has said, "waits all night under the George Washington Bridge for George to keep a scholarly rendezvous with her, which of course he fails to do."[15] Ostriker, professor emeritus at Rutgers University, is herself a poet and has written a fine poem titled "The Bridge." While the early stanzas are not concerned with the George except perhaps metaphorically, the final stanza is, and is a joy:

Some snowflakes whip across the lanes of cars
Slowed for the tollbooth, and two smoky gulls
Veer by the steel parabolas.
Given a choice of tunnel or bridge
Into Manhattan, the granite crust
On its black platter of rivers, we prefer
Elevation to depth, vista to crawling.[16]

Perhaps the finest of the poems dedicated to the G.W.B. is by Israel Newman, an immigrant from Lithuania. Try as I may, I cannot find a title or bibliographic information on the poem. It was published, sans title, in a book by Julius Henry Cohen, longtime general counsel of the Port Authority, *They Builded Better than They Knew:*

Here strings are cables, harps a bridge
From concrete cliffs to those of granite;
Here where the Hudson feels the sea
Iron is music built upon it.
Go sail beneath this mile-long arch
Of steel and traffic, hear it drone
Tremendous music, you will find
Its iron hymn the city's own.[17]

The line "Here where the Hudson feels the sea" is beautifully suggestive of the G.W.B.'s site, not to mention a welcome corrective to Donald Westlake's confusing the Hudson with the ocean.

Children's Literature

I have discovered three children's books in which the George Washington Bridge is central, but I want to mention three others where the George receives consideration. *Harry's Helicopter,* by Joan Anderson, is about a boy who fashions a cardboard helicopter that takes off in a wind gust with him in it. Learning to steer, he follows two gulls over the George Washington Bridge.[18] *Fireboat: The Heroic Adventures of the John J. Harvey,* by Maira Kalman, concerns the congruence of the launching of this famous fireboat in 1931 with the inauguration of the G.W.B. that same year. Retired in 1994, the *Harvey* was pressed back into service on 9/11, its powerful pumps providing Hudson River water to the smoldering Twin Towers site.[19] Finally, in his book *Reaching for the Moon,* astronaut Buzz Aldrin, a New Jersey native, attributes his courage and skill in landing on the moon to such earlier adventures as biking across the George Washington Bridge alone at the age of ten.[20]

Of the three children's books I'll discuss in detail, two are famous, the other little known. The latter is Manus Pinkwater's *Wingman,* which concerns a lonely Chinese American boy, Donald, who lives in Washington Heights and often plays hookey from school because the other children call him "a dumb chinky Chinaman." On most days he climbs up into the New York tower of the George Washington Bridge, where, sitting on a girder, he reads comic books all day. One day, Wingman flies up into the bridge and lands on Donald's girder. Donald, whose last name is Wing, is astounded when he notices that this superhero is Chinese just like him. One day Wingman carries Donald from the G.W.B. to China, where the boy develops respect for his ethnic heritage. On his return to school he draws wonderful pictures of life in China that intrigue his teacher and win his classmates' respect.[21]

My favorite children's book in which the George Washington plays an important role is Faith Ringgold's *Tar Beach.* Despite being one of America's most celebrated folk artists today, Ringgold has had to combat four distinct prejudices in her career. The first two involved being African American and being a female artist. The third has had to do with her often working in fabrics rather than on canvas—the accusation that she is a "craftsperson" rather than an artist. Writing and illustrating children's books is the fourth. "Some people think illustrators are a lower form of life," she says. Happily, the *New York Times* didn't think so when they created "A Literary Map of Manhattan." The second item on their list was Ringgold's childhood neighborhood, where *Tar Beach* takes place.[22]

The first of Ringgold's eleven children's books, *Tar Beach* was awarded the Caldecott Medal. Much of it is adapted from one of her five "Woman on a Bridge" brightly painted and pieced quilts. (Another of them, "Dancing on the George Washington Bridge," decorates the back of my own book's jacket.) On the original "Tar Beach" quilt is found much of the text of the children's book, inked as a border. The central figure is Cassie, based on Ringgold's memories of her childhood. To escape the sweltering summer heat of a Harlem apartment, her family would in the evening go up to their "beach" on the roof. From there they would stare at the lights of the George Washington Bridge. For Cassie, "the bridge was my most prized possession." Her great desire is to someday fly over the George Washington Bridge, and one evening she does just that. "Now I have claimed it," she says. "I can wear it like a giant diamond necklace."

Flying is an important motif in much of Ringgold's work, a metaphor for freedom. Her autobiography is titled *We Flew over the Bridge,* and one of her children's books is titled *Aunt Harriet's Underground Railroad in the Sky.* "Flying is about believing you can do anything you set your mind to and then doing it," she says. "Flying is pursuing your dreams."[23]

Ringgold has been a G.W.B. aficionado her whole life. She was actually born in 1930, but Cassie says in *Tar Beach* that she was born on the very day the George Washington opened in 1931. Ringgold now lives in Englewood, New Jersey, not far down the road from the bridge. "I would never want to be more than three minutes from the George," she says. Ringgold says she loves the George Washington Bridge especially because "I could always see it as I grew up. That bridge has been in my life for as long as I can remember. As a kid, I could walk across it anytime I chose. I love to see it sparkling in the night. I moved to New Jersey and I'm still next to it."[24] Recently, she had installed a mosaic of the "Tar Beach" quilt on the outside of her home. In years to come it will no doubt become a place of artistic pilgrimage for admirers of both the George Washington Bridge and Faith Ringgold's work.

No doubt the most famous children's book about the George Washington Bridge is *The Little Red Lighthouse and the Great Gray Bridge,* written by Hildegarde Swift, with illustrations by Lynd Ward. Published in 1942 and with sales over the years in the millions, it is still in print. It has also inspired a short film, with the book's pictures providing the principal visuals, a narrator reading the book's text, and music and sound effects rounding out the total experience.[25]

The book is based on the little red lighthouse (only forty feet high) that stands at the base of the New York Tower and was briefly discussed in chapter 1. The little lighthouse is proud that it saves boats from disaster with its beam. But then: "Every day it watched the strange new gray thing beside it grow and grow. Huge towers seemed to touch the sky. Strong loops of steel swept across the river. It made the little red lighthouse feel very, very small." When a great light, no doubt the Will Rogers–Wiley Post beacon, is placed atop the New York tower, the little red lighthouse thinks, "Now I am no longer needed. My light is so little and this one so big!" The old man who turned on the little red lighthouse each evening comes no more. One day, though, there is a great storm, with thick fog, and a tugboat, which is accustomed to seeing the little red lighthouse's beacon and can't see the bridge's because it is aimed at the sky, crashes on the rocks. Unable to help, the little red lighthouse was "VERY, VERY SAD."

But then

the great gray bridge called to the little red lighthouse: "Little brother, where is your light?"

"Am I brother of yours, bridge?" wondered the lighthouse. "Your light was so bright that I thought mine was needed no more."

"I call to the airplanes," cried the bridge. "I flash to the ships of the air. But you are still master of the river. Quick, let your light shine again. Each to his own place, little brother."

Given the emergency, the old man arrives and turns on the lighthouse equipment, and the rest of the boats going by are saved. The book ends thus: "And now beside the great beacon of the bridge the small beam of the lighthouse still flashes. Beside the towering gray bridge the lighthouse still bravely stands. Though it knows now that it is little, it is still VERY, VERY PROUD." It's easy to see the immense appeal of the book to children, who are assured that, while small, they are still important.

The Jeffrey's Hook lighthouse, the subject of the famous children's book *The Little Red Lighthouse and the Great Gray Bridge*. The lighthouse is in Fort Washington Park, immediately beneath the New York tower. Courtesy of Dave Frieder.

In fact, since the building of the G.W.B., with elaborate lights affixed to the New York tower at water's edge, the lighthouse is never lit. However, it remains important as the locale of the annual Little Red Lighthouse Festival, attended by hundreds of parents and their children and featuring food, kiddie rides, arts and crafts, and balloons. You can climb to the top of the lighthouse, and, as the highlight of the festival, a celebrity reads the book aloud; past readers have included James Earl Jones, Bette Midler, and Pete Seeger. After hiking across the bridge from Fort Lee on September 16, 2006, I attended the event. That year's reader was the tiny immigrant sexologist Dr. Ruth Westheimer. At the conclusion of her reading she got all present—many of us seemed to know the book by heart—to join her in loudly reciting the final words, "VERY, VERY PROUD."

Afterward, I interviewed Dr. Ruth briefly.[26] I learned that she has lived in the same Washington Heights apartment, close to the George Washington Bridge, for more than half a century. Joking with her, I asked if she thought the little red lighthouse was a phallic symbol. Not missing a beat, she responded, referencing Freud, "Darlink, dere are times ven a cigar is choost a cigar."

Valeri Larko's painting of the underside of the G.W.B. from the perspective
of the New Jersey shore, 1992. Courtesy of the artist.

The George Washington Bridge in the Other Arts

ALL ALONG, I HAVE BEEN ARGUING that the George Washington Bridge is a work of art of a special kind. As one commentator has put it, Othmar Ammann "found in New York the perfect setting for his artistic expression, where his works could span masses of land and be written across the sky."[1] The G.W.B. also has a symbiotic relationship with the arts. It inspires artistic expression, and that expression, in turn, affects how we look at the bridge.

Movies

The George Washington Bridge, like the Manhattan skyline, the Brooklyn Bridge, and the Statue of Liberty, is one of the familiar images filmmakers use simply to establish that we are approaching or near New York City.[2] For example, in the Tom Hanks film *Big* (1988), there is a distant view of the bridge in the scene with the "Zoltar Speaks" fortune-telling machine. In the opening of *When Harry Met Sally* (1989), with Billy Crystal and Meg Ryan, a car is tracked across the G.W.B. on its way into the city. In *Frequency* (2000), with Dennis Quaid, what purports to be an off-ramp of the bridge is used to stage a horrendous accident and fire involving a fuel truck. In *Michael Clayton* (2007), the bridge is twice used in the background to establish that the George Clooney character is driving on the Henry Hudson Parkway.

In *The Godfather* (1972), a car with Michael Corleone and some mobsters in it passes a sign on a bridge that says TO NEW JERSEY. A number of sources indicate that this is the G.W.B., but even though that is where the action is meant to be taking place, the scene had to have been shot on a fabricated set or another bridge. There is no such sign on either level of the George Washington Bridge, and it is impossible to make a U-turn on the G.W.B. like the one that occurs in the scene.

Another film in which the bridge itself is not shown but is thematically important is *Network* (1976), which garnered virtually every major Oscar. In this early send-up of television, Max Schumacher (William Holden), head of the network's News Division, repeatedly tells this story about it: "I said to this cabdriver, 'Take me to the middle of the George Washington Bridge.' We were supposed to do a remote from there. It was 1962. They had just finished the Lower Deck. But the cabbie said, 'Don't do it, buddy. You're young. You have your whole life ahead of you.'"[3]

In a few films, important scenes take place on and around the George. Having concluded the previous chapter with *The Little Red Lighthouse and the Great Gray Bridge,* I'll first mention two in which the lighthouse and the underbridge area on the New York side play a role—a very different role than in the beloved book.

The first is the 1948 noir classic *Force of Evil* starring John Garfield as Joe Morse, a crooked lawyer in the employ of the mob. Thomas Gomez plays his honest brother Leo, who refuses to cooperate with the criminals. A mobster phones Joe Morse and tells him that his brother is "on the rocks by the lighthouse under the bridge." Unsure what he will find there, Joe rushes down the great staircase off Riverside Drive saying, in voiceover, "It was like going down to the bottom of the world." Hurrying under the New York tower and past the lighthouse, he finds Leo dead at water's edge. Cradling his body, Joe vows to lead a blameless life thenceforth and starts on his new path by turning himself in to the police. There is wonderful black-and-white footage of the George Washington Bridge towers, the underside of the bridge, Jeffrey's Hook, and the lighthouse.[4]

The second is the 2003 suspense film *In the Cut*. It has a number of extended shots of both levels of the G.W.B. and includes a trip across the bridge to New Jersey and back. A serial murderer in New York City is killing women, including the half sister of Frannie Avery (Meg Ryan). Frannie begins to suspect her lover, homicide detective Malloy (Mark Ruffalo). But his partner, Detective Rodriguez (Nick Damici), whom

Frannie trusts and confides in, is the killer. The long climactic scene takes place at the lighthouse, to whose cast-iron fence and interior Rodriguez has personal access. On a romantic pretense, he takes Frannie there, puts on dreamy music—he's installed a stereo system—and asks her to dance. It slowly dawns on her that Rodriguez is the killer and that this is the place where he has carved up his several victims. She's next, but she cleverly overcomes him and, bedraggled, makes her way up to Riverside Drive and hitches a ride downtown.[5]

The first movie in which the George Washington Bridge played a role appeared ten years after the bridge was inaugurated: 1941's screwball comedy *Ball of Fire,* starring Gary Cooper as Professor Bertram Potts and Barbara Stanwyck as Sugarpuss O'Shea. Potts and seven other fuddy-duddy professors have been compiling for nine years an encyclopedia of "all human knowledge," and Potts's specialty is language. In the interest of understanding slang, he enlists O'Shea, an entertainer and gang moll. Sugarpuss is supposed to marry a mobster who has outwitted the New York police by escaping with his gang to New Jersey. Sugarpuss enlists the professors to drive her there, presumably as part of their education in slang but really to provide her a legitimate cover. The professors cross the George Washington Bridge, crashing into a truck at a tollbooth on the New Jersey side. (Until 1970 tolls were collected both ways on the bridge.) Meanwhile, Potts has fallen in love with Sugarpuss and she with him. In the nick of time, the professors outwit the mobsters, true love triumphs, and the professors drive happily back across the George Washington Bridge.[6]

How to Marry a Millionaire (1953) also has characteristics of the screwball comedy. It concerns three gold-digger models, played by Marilyn Monroe, Betty Grable, and Lauren Bacall, who come to New York determined to snare rich husbands. The one played by Betty Grable goes away to Maine with an extremely wealthy gentleman. No sparks fly between them. On their return to New York, on what looks like the Palisades Parkway, they approach the bridge. The man wishes to slip quietly back into New York because he is actually married. However, his is the fifty millionth car to cross the G.W.B. Once they are through the tollbooths, motorcycle police pull alongside as an escort. Reaching New York, to the consternation of the philandering man, they are greeted by dignitaries and the press.[7]

In *Desperately Seeking Susan,* a 1985 film starring Madonna and Roseanna Arquette, Roberta Glass (Arquette), is a bored suburban housewife; even her husband calls her "the straightest person in Fort Lee." While hosting a party in her Palisades high-rise, she gazes longingly at the George Washington Bridge, lit in all its nighttime finery. She sees it as her escape route to an exciting life just across the Hudson River in Manhattan. Soon she does exactly that: crosses the G.W.B. in pursuit of adventure.

Susan (Madonna) is a disreputable party girl we first see in an Atlantic City bedroom scene and then on a bus crossing the George Washington Bridge. She alights at the G.W.B. Bus Station and goes downstairs to take the subway. In a club where she once worked, the hatcheck girl asks, "Where were you? We thought you were dead." Susan answers, "Nah, just over in Jersey." Through a complicated mix-up, Roberta assumes Susan's identity. Crossing the George Washington Bridge has transformed her. She throws herself into life in Manhattan, which is portrayed as wild and exciting. At the end of the film Roberta isn't sure what she is going to do with herself, but it would appear that returning to Fort Lee isn't an option. Whatever she does will likely be on the east side of the George.[8]

Probably the most important film in which the George Washington Bridge, as well as its immediate neighborhood, plays an important role is *Cop Land* (1997), a story about crooked New York City police who live across the Hudson in tiny Garrison, New Jersey, population 1,280. The fictional Garrison is based on Edgewater, a town just south of the bridge on the banks of the Hudson, mentioned in chapter 7 in connection with a bridge suicide. Much of the film was shot there and in nearby Cliffside Park. The George Washington Bridge is in view much of the time, representing the frontier between two civilizations: sophisticated but corrupt New York City and ordinary but wholesome New Jersey.

The Lower Level is the set for the opening scene. A young off-duty policeman, Babitch, driving home to Garrison on the bridge, is challenged by two Hispanics and kills them. Babitch's uncle Ray (Harvey Keitel) is the leader of the crooked cops. He plants a gun and cocaine in the dead men's car and fixes things so it appears Babitch, in remorse over their deaths, jumped off the bridge. "Hero Cop," the *Daily News* headlines. Ray hides Babitch. He doesn't want an investigation that might jeopardize the sweet deal he and the other Garrison police enjoy. He says, "We cross the bridge every day to go to work. Here we made a place for our families where they could live good. Nothin's getting in the way."

But Moe Tilden (Robert De Niro), a lieutenant in the N.Y.P.D. Internal Affairs Division, has long suspected something crooked is going on among the police who live in Garrison. He knows that the financing for their homes was provided by two mob-controlled banks. Now he is struck by the fact that "nobody saw a body hit the water." Tilden has a problem, though: "Half the people I'm watching in this job live over there, but my jurisdiction ends at the G.W. Bridge." He needs the help of the Garrison sheriff, Freddie Heflin (Sylvester Stallone), an honest, plain-spoken, hardworking officer—no genius, but not slick either. He is definitely a small-town Jersey boy: he looks longingly at the George Washington Bridge outside his window; he listens to a lot of Bruce Springsteen.

Heflin admires the police living in his town and wishes he could be a "real policeman" too, but he cannot be admitted to their ranks because he is deaf in one ear. He has never before imagined that they could be crooked. Now, suspecting that Babitch is very much alive, Heflin begins to put two and two together. He also finally understands the connection between how on the New York side of the river "the mob gets to run all the drugs it wants" while on his side of the river "everyone gets a nice house."

New Jersey towns do not have sheriffs (sheriff is a county function), but James Mangold, who wrote and directed *Cop Land,* wanted to make an urban western, and New Jersey has sometimes been seen, and is embodied here by Freddy Heflin, as the beginning of the American West. One of the finest ongoing rodeos in America is in Woodstown, New Jersey. There are suggestions of the classic western *High Noon* in *Cop Land,* with Freddie fighting all the bad guys alone in the streets; as in *High Noon,* there are also shots of a ticking clock to heighten the tension. In the end, against immense odds, the heroic, wounded Heflin captures Babitch, who is "the evidence" needed to lock up all the crooked cops, and spirits him across the Hudson to Tilden's office.[9]

Theater, Television, and Video

The George does not loom large in the theatrical landscape. Various plays mention "the bridge and tunnel crowd"—a somewhat disparaging reference to those people, principally suburban New Jerseyans, who come to Manhattan for weekend recreation, and a one-woman play written and performed by Sarah Jones is called *Bridge and Tunnel.*

In *480 East 50th,* one of the main characters, Edward, commits suicide by jumping off the George Washington Bridge.[10] *Land of Dreams* traces the Romeo and Juliet–like dueling-ethnicities romance of Daniel Sussman, an Orthodox Jew, and Gina Zagara, the Italian girl next door, from the time they are thirteen until, at nineteen, after their high school prom, Daniel proposes marriage to Gina on the G.W.B.[11] In the Broadway musical *In the Heights* (it is Washington Heights that is referenced), which opened in 2008, the George Washington Bridge is mentioned in one song, and a giant photograph of the bridge is in the background looming over the set.[12]

On television the bridge has been used many times for scenes in which the police are chasing crooks, but its finest moment is an *I Love Lucy* episode in which the four main characters embark on a cross-country trip singing "California, Here We Come" as they drive across.[13]

The G.W.B. is the subject of a rather ingenious haiku-video by Maurice Peterson set to the music of John Coltrane.[14] Peterson lived for many years in Washington Heights overlooking the bridge and says that it was "my daily inspiration, the icon of everything special about New York, the very essence of the kind of magic mankind sometimes makes." The short but beautiful text follows:

> George Washington Bridge
> Diamonds in my window
> Necklace of the clouds

Painting

I want to begin by returning to Faith Ringgold's work, which I discussed in the children's literature section of the previous chapter. Ringgold is represented in the collections of many of the great museums of America, including the Metropolitan Museum of Art, the Guggenheim, and the Museum of Modern Art in New York, as well as in the private collections of such luminaries as Oprah Winfrey, Bill Cosby, and Maya Angelou, and she has been awarded seventeen honorary degrees. She is certainly a great artist, and no bridge has been better celebrated in any medium than the G.W.B. is in her five-part "Woman on the Bridge" series story quilts and her beautiful children's book *Tar Beach.* In her own way, she has done for the George what Joseph Stella did for the Brooklyn, even if sewn art and illustration continue to fight for their place in the sun.

The original "Tar Beach" quilt painting (1988) by Faith Ringgold, with the family camped out on their rooftop beach and Cassie flying over the George Washington. This work appears as the cover illustration of her book *Tar Beach*. Faith Ringgold © 1988. Courtesy of the artist.

George Ault (1891–1948) was a painter very much in the Charles Sheeler precisionist mode that, especially in the 1920s and 1930s, embraced Machine Age aesthetics. It focused on architecture and engineering, seeing them as mankind's salvation, and disputed America's continued dedication to what it considered the "agrarian myth." One of Ault's major paintings, *The George Washington Bridge,* is celebrated for its order, clarity, and dreamlike quality. His works have been shown at the Whitney Museum of American Art in New York and are found in the collection of the Smithsonian American Art Museum in Washington.

Valeri Larko's talent is in lending human thoughts and feelings to industrial subjects. This she accomplishes especially in her painting *G.W. Bridge,* which is focused on the dark underside of the bridge, with the lower portions of the New Jersey tower foregrounded and the rest of the bridge sweeping away to the east. As she put it to me, "In all of my artwork, I am interested in the often overlooked view of things. This is why I chose to paint underneath the bridge looking up at it instead of the more traditional approach of a direct view. There's also a sense of power and immensity that you get from something as massive as the G.W.B., especially when you spend several weeks painting underneath it."[15] In 2000, Larko was commissioned by New Jersey Transit and the New Jersey State Council on the Arts to paint four murals depicting New Jersey engineering wonders for the new Secaucus Transfer Station, the largest railroad station in the state, which opened in 2003.

Photography

Art photographers have long been interested in the George Washington Bridge because of its bold architectural features. Some of Edward Steichen's (1879–1973) finest photographs were taken on the G.W.B. Steichen, who served as director of the Department of Photography of the Museum of Modern Art in New York City, was a major figure in American art history, helping to make photography celebrated not just for its documentary possibilities but as an art form in its own right.

In recent years photography of the bridge has been hampered by two factors. One is that for nine years one tower or the other was wrapped as part of the lead abatement and repainting project. In that form they may have appealed to the artist Christo but, I am reasonably sure, to no one else. The other, of course, is that in our post-9/11 world all photography of large, indispensable structures such as the G.W.B. is regarded with suspicion if not entirely forbidden. Thus it has been, of late, near impossible to get fine pictures of the bridge.

Dave Frieder, also known as "the Bridge Man," is forever climbing bridges and taking pictures of their most intimate features. For years he's been working on a book of photographs of New York bridges, most taken from high up on their towers. The George Washington especially attracts him, and his pictures of it are found in many books on bridges, including my own. "I love bridges in general," he says, "but the George Washington will always, for me, reign supreme."[16] Frieder is one person whose ongoing work has been immensely affected by the unavailability or limited access to his favorite haunts.

This is also true of Steven Siegel, who in photography shares some of the same interests Valeri Larko has in painting—that is, squeezing meaning and pathos out of inanimate objects and forcing the viewer of his work to see the manufactured landscape from a new perspective. Siegel's photographs are also represented in this book. Siegel told me, "I've always loved suspension bridges. As a kid I would ask my parents, on my birthday, to drive me around the New York metropolitan area and visit all of the major bridges. My fascination with bridges continues to this day. And the George is the most stirring of all."[17]

Music

Aaron Copland's "Symphonic Ode," composed in 1929, is music evoked by the sounds of the G.W.B. under construction. Listening carefully, you hear instruments imitating rivet-drivers and jackhammers.

William Schuman's 7 1/2 minute "George Washington Bridge," which he classified as "An Impression for Band," is the most important music so far inspired by the G.W.B. A rousing, quick-paced number, it was created in 1950 by the eminent composer, who served as president of the Juilliard School (1945–1962) and of Lincoln Center (1962–1969) and was awarded the first Pulitzer Prize for music (1943).[18]

"I lived in Englewood and walked across . . . [the G.W.B.] just after it was opened to pedestrians," Schuman said. "I always loved it. There are few days in the year when I do not see the George Washington Bridge. I pass it on my way to work as I drive along the Henry Hudson Parkway on the New York shore. Ever since my student days, when I watched the progress of its construction, this bridge has had for me an almost human personality, and this personality is astonishingly varied, assuming different moods depending on the time of day or night, the weather, the traffic, and, of course, my own mood as I pass by.

"I have walked across it late at night when it was shrouded in fog and during the brilliant sunshine hours of midday. I have driven over it countless times and passed under it in boats. Coming to New York City by air, sometimes I have been lucky enough to fly over it. It is difficult to imagine a more gracious welcome or dramatic entry to the great metropolis."[19]

Often, when I've told people of a certain age that I was writing a book on the bridge, they have broken into a silly song repeating the words "George Washington Bridge" over and over. None of them could remember where the song had originated. Sometimes they would vary the song with "George Washington's bridge," a reference to the first president's dentures, often incorrectly described as made of wood.

One of the singers pointed me to a conversation between Ernie and Bert on *Sesame Street* that went like this.

> ERNIE: If George Washington was going to New Jersey, why didn't he do what everybody does?
> BERT: What's that, Ernie?
> ERNIE: Take the George Washington Bridge, Bert!

The conversation led me to look further into *Sesame Street*. I thought I had finally tracked down the origins of the song when I discovered a 1982 *Sesame Street Sing-Along* record with its opening lyrics:

> BERT: I got one! (*He sings the A-B-C*)
> ERNIE: Or . . ." George Washington Bridge! George Washington Washington Bridge. George Washington Bridge. George Washington Washington Bridge." Here comes the sad part. (*sobbing*) "George Washington Bridge. George Washington Washington Bridge . . ."
> BERT: Ernie . . .
> ERNIE: But it ends really happy, Bert. "George Washington Bridge! George Washington Washington Bridge!"

I was content with this explanation for the silly song's origins until the day in 2007, while having my annual physical exam, I happened to mention to my doctor, Gary Weine, that I was writing this book and he immediately burst into song. His version was somewhat different from Ernie and Bert's:

> George Washington Bridge
> George Washington Washington Bridge
> > George ...
> > George ...
> > George ...
> > > Washington Bridge

I asked him if he had gotten the song from *Sesame Street*.

"Absolutely not!" he said. "The song is way before *Sesame Street*. My Uncle Seymour, a real card, would sing the song when he got to the bridge and keep singing it until he had crossed it. Uncle Seymour and Aunt Esther had no children of their own, so they would often take me places in their car. We'd usually go across the George Washington Bridge, and he'd always sing it and everyone in the car would join in. Then, when my kids were young, I'd sing it when we crossed the bridge and they'd sing along with me. It's a family tradition. If I called up my Aunt Esther right now—she's eighty-five—she'd burst out laughing and sing along with me."

"So who made it up?"

"What do you mean, who made it up?" he replied. "Uncle Seymour made it up!" Then he added, doubt creeping into his voice: "Didn't he?"

For all I know, Uncle Seymour did make it up. It's as good an explanation as any other. In any case, I hereby announce my retirement from the investigation. Having discharged my responsibilities as best I could, I invite readers to take up the search for the song's origins on their own. I shall be happy to hear the results; you can e-mail me at rockland@rci.rutgers.edu. New revelations about the song will be acknowledged in any subsequent editions of this book.

The bridge photographed from the New Jersey tower looking toward Manhattan. Walkways can be discerned on both north and south sides just beyond the roadway. Courtesy of the Local History Department, The Morristown and Morris Township Public Library.

10

Life Along the Walkways

THE GEORGE WASHINGTON BRIDGE has inspired much art, but none of it offers quite the aesthetic pleasure, not to mention the adventure, of being on the bridge itself. This is especially true on the walkways, where everything is slowed down and you find yourself not so much on the bridge as in it. Unlike motorists, who often frantically cross the bridge unaware the walkways exist, those on the walkways are relaxed, unconcerned about rushing vehicles or about when and where to exit.

The G.W.B. has two walkways, both on the Upper Level, one on the north side, one on the south. They're a little difficult to access. On the New Jersey side, as I said earlier, both are just off Hudson Terrace in Fort Lee. On the Manhattan side, you get to them at 178th St. and 179th Street and Cabrini Boulevard.

The walkways are urban recreation spaces available to everyone. There is no better place to enjoy the Hudson River, the Palisades, and New York City, and to do so as you wish—whether strolling, hiking, skating, jogging, or biking. I regularly encounter New Yorkers and New Jerseyans surprised to learn that you can cross the George Washington Bridge under your own power. If you are normally an armchair traveler, please put down this book and take a walk on the bridge at your earliest opportunity. Just think: you can walk to another state—and in the most dramatic fashion.

Indeed, if you'd like, you can have one foot in one state, one foot in the other. Children especially delight in doing this. State-line signs are posted on both levels. On the Upper Level, they are mounted on the outside of the walkways facing traffic. A legend I remember from boyhood days is that there is a policeman posted at the state line wearing a uniform half of which is a New York state policeman's, the other half a New Jersey state policeman's. I'm not sure I've entirely stopped looking for that phantom policeman yet.

Another pleasure in walking across the G.W.B. is the novelty of crossing it without paying the customary high toll exacted when you drive, six dollars round-trip in 2007 but going to rise to eight dollars in 2008.[1] As you may remember, when the bridge opened in 1931 there were tolls for pedestrians and bikers too; young children were free. As many as 150,000 pedestrians used the bridge annually in the 1930s (I've discovered no use figures for bikers), and the bridge took in as much as $11,000 in annual revenues from them. In 1934, tolls for pedestrians were reduced from ten cents to five cents. Then, in 1940, they were eliminated for both pedestrians and bikers. This must be one of the rare instances in history when tolls have been reduced and even done away with.[2]

Each bridge walkway is ten feet wide, though narrowed by almost three feet at those points where the suspender cables, descending from the barrel cables, pass through the deck in groups of four on both sides of the walkway. It's too bad the walkways are not wider; benches every hundred yards would be a real amenity. More people would be attracted to the walkways, especially the elderly. Instead of the bridge being only something to pass over, it would be a destination to be enjoyed for itself and its magnificent views.

Where the suspender cables pass through, the walkways have been further reduced by another foot since 9/11 by the steel "blast shields" or "security casings" (some bridge staffers call them one thing, some the other) wrapped around each suspender cable to minimize if not nullify the effects of explosive devices. As part of the general "hardening" of the bridge, the blast shields are particularly elaborate at its center, where the barrel cables curve down to a height only fifteen feet above the road surface. The blast shields at this point rise up to also encase the barrel cables themselves with what bridge staff refer to as "knuckles." A large explosion here, were the barrel cables unprotected, could place the whole bridge in jeopardy.

In the past, except when construction projects compromised one side of the bridge, both walkways were available at all times, but since 9/11 only one at a time has been open to the public. It has generally been the south walkway, because it is accessible on either end via a ramp, whereas both ends of the north walkway are accessible only via a series of switchbacking staircases. The staircases include grooved steel rails for bikers to push their bikes up or down the stairs, but most serious bikers ignore them, being able to move more quickly on the steps with their lightweight bikes hoisted shoulder high.

Recently, because of work being done on the south walkway, it was the north walkway that was open. The north allows an unrestricted view of the Palisades upriver from Fort Lee, but the south offers a much better view of Manhattan's great buildings. Would that it were possible to cross the bridge on one walkway and return on the other. That is what my friends and I did when we were boys, hiking on one walkway from New York to the Palisades to camp out, returning the next day on the other.

In August 2004, walkway accessibility was compromised further when New York City police, for "security reasons" never fully explained to bridge officials, asked that the walkways be closed entirely during the Republican National Convention, held in Manhattan's Madison Square Garden. General manager Bob Durando told me the police had some notion demonstrations might take place on the bridge, but given its distance from the convention, approximately eight miles, this would have been unlikely—although certainly a demonstration on the bridge that blocked traffic would have received a good deal of attention in the media. Revelations in 2007 suggested that New York City police, under pressure from a Republican National Committee so-called Intelligence Squad—citing concerns about "terrorism" when it was clearly embarrassment that worried them—may indeed, in violation of the Constitution, have tried to head off any kind of demonstration in the Greater New York City area during the convention.[3]

Bridge officials refused to close the walkway, citing the needs of commuting bikers, but they did limit hours so that it was closed from 9:00 P.M. through 6:00 A.M., and those hours remained in effect until shortly after the convention was over. The walkway has been open ever since except from midnight to 5:00 A.M. I asked a security guard posted on the bridge: why close at all? "Jumpers," he said. "We can't see them in the dark, wouldn't be able to stop them."

This made no sense to me; obviously, it's dark before midnight and after five all year. Bob Durando agreed. He told me the guard was "simply misinformed. Because of other security needs, we just don't have the resources to keep a walkway open 24/7, so we close it during the hours it's least used." Durando sympathizes with those who are inconvenienced. "I know bikers and pedestrians aren't happy," he says, but "these days security trumps everything else. If someone knocked down the George, life in this part of the world—the economy, transportation, communications—would be infinitely more disrupted than it was after 9/11. The region is recovering from the loss of the Twin Towers. I don't know how it could recover if we lost the George."

I asked Durando what would happen if someone climbed over the gates and got onto one of the closed walkways. "We would know almost immediately and they would be taken into custody," he said.[4]

One evening on the walkway, I met Ralph Casey, who lives in Washington Heights. He told me that those early morning hours had been the very time he frequented the bridge. "I'm an insomniac," he said. "I used to take a walk on the bridge nearly every night between 2:00 and 3:00 A.M. It's beautiful then, quiet and safe—not like the city streets. The walk would calm me down and I'd go home and sleep. Now I take Seconal. Why should I be forced to take sleeping pills when all I need is a walk on the bridge?"[5]

Pedestrians, joggers, and bikers with whom I spoke believe that at least one walkway should be open twenty-four hours a day. Indeed, many expressed their disappointment that both walkways are not open round the clock. Casey feels that way. "Why should the road be open for traffic 24/7 and not both walkways?" he asks. "It doesn't make sense. If the concern is security, aren't vehicles, maybe with bombs in them, more dangerous than pedestrians?"

Most people I spoke with on the walkways also favored restricting one walkway to pedestrians, joggers, and skaters and the other to bikers, or confining everyone heading east to one walkway, everyone heading west to the other. One biker said the only thing he feared biking across the bridge was a head-on collision with another bike. "Sometimes I imagine it and it freaks me out," he said. "The other biker and I hit, and I go flying over my handlebars. I get scuffed up on the walkway and maybe break my arm. That's if I'm lucky. But if we collide just so, I get launched over the inside roadway railing and end up under an eighteen-wheeler or I catapult over the outside railing and fall to the river below. Either way I'm dead."[6]

Bicycles are what pedestrians and joggers on the walkways fear most. "You can't have bikes and people on foot in the same place," one pedestrian said to me. "Where am I supposed to go when there's a biker right behind me and he's impatient? And maybe there's another bike coming the other way so he can't pass me?" There are faded signs on the walkway indicating which side bikers should use, which pedestrians, and others (in English and Spanish) urging bikers to respect pedestrians, but they are largely ignored. There are no signs concerning roller skaters, who tend to weave side to side as they move, making pedestrians, joggers, and bikers unhappy. So, pedestrians and joggers are occasionally angry with bikers, bikers with pedestrians and joggers, and all of them with skaters and with bridge authorities.

Nevertheless, the people I have met on the bridge walkways almost always seem to be in good spirits. In my experience, that's generally true of people who embrace exercise and the out-of-doors. I've never met a mean-spirited hiker. And those on the bridge walkways enjoy a sense that they're special, doing something many people do not know about, much less do. They're urban adventurers. A fellow named Eric Hollander had only been biking to work briefly when I spoke with him but had noticed, "Every time I ride my bike I'm in a good mood all day. And the best part is the bridge. It's like the boardwalk at the beach when I'm on the walkway."[7]

Denis Finnin, a professional photographer, lives in Weehawken, New Jersey, and has been commuting by bike to work in midtown Manhattan for eight years. He showers when he gets there and changes into the fresh clothes he carries in his backpack, returning home at the end of the week with his laundry. Denis also considers the George Washington Bridge the best part of the trip: "I've been on the bridge when it was mysteriously beautiful with fog swirling about the towers. I've seen the river almost completely blocked with ice floes. You can glimpse these things from cars, but you can't stop and marvel at them. At night I'm often returning to New Jersey as the sun sets in the west and the sky and bridge are magical.

"I'm on 'vacation' an hour each morning and evening. How many people can say that? Not to mention that, by biking to work, I get the satisfaction of doing a little something for the environment. The days I can't commute by bike—maybe because there's been a blizzard or an ice storm—seem to drag. In fact, whenever I haven't been on the bike enough my wife says, 'You're getting cranky, go for a ride.' But most days, with the rides to look forward to, I'm happy. I'm in my fifties, but I feel like a kid. It really has a positive effect on my work, too. I focus. Heck, commuting by bike you learn to focus or you don't stay alive very long."

Denis confesses to having had a few minor accidents commuting to work, but not on the bridge. "For example, I'm coming along a street in Manhattan near my office and suddenly a person in a parked car opens their door. For a biker, there's nothing worse than getting doored."[8]

Pearl Perkins is also a photographer and a biker, but she travels in the opposite direction. Pearl lives in Manhattan and since 1998 has worked for a publishing company in Englewood Cliffs, New Jersey, just north of Fort Lee. Six months after taking the job, she began commuting five days a week by bike. "If there's thirty inches of snow or bad ice I won't do it," she says, "but otherwise I never miss a day. No matter how hot or cold or how hard it's raining, I go." Unlike Denis Finnin, however, Pearl has no

Denis Finnin commutes to Manhattan on his bicycle from his home in Weehawken, New Jersey. Courtesy of Andy Lausten.

shower facilities awaiting at her job. "So I go into the ladies' room and take 'a bird bath' in the sink. And I also bring fresh clothes every day in my backpack and bring them home with me at the end of the day."

Pearl grew up in Germany, where she started riding a bicycle to school in the first grade and never stopped. "It means even more to me now than when I was a little girl because now I'm working all day in a studio, with artificial light and artificial air. The bridge is my antidote."

One night, during the brief period in 2004 when the walkway closed at 9:00 P.M., Pearl had to work till 10:00 P.M. in Englewood Cliffs. When she got to the bridge, the walkway was blocked. This did not entirely shock her. "It seems like they're always closing the walkways and changing the hours without warning," she said. What Pearl did was lift her bike over the railing into the slowest of the four eastbound roadway lanes and ride across the G.W.B. to Manhattan amid the motor traffic. "I didn't ask if I could do it," she says. "I've learned that you don't ask about such things. If you ask, there's always someone who says no."

"Were you scared?" I asked.

"Very," she said, "but I had to get home. Luckily, the bridge is well lit. But cars kept honking at me as if I was some kind of alien life form. Crossing the bridge that night was a very long mile." Ironically, when the George Washington Bridge opened in 1931—of course, with far fewer and slower-moving motor vehicles—bicycles, considered in the same category as motorcycles, were restricted to the road surface.

This policy remained in effect for many years. I've been unable to determine whether it was ever changed formally or whether, for safety's sake, bikers gravitated to the walkways and by now riding there is customary. As recently as 1977, when I arrived at the tollbooths on my bicycle toward the end of a two-day trip, there seemed to be uncertainty as to where bikes were to go. I did not know what the rules were for crossing the bridge by bike, nor did I remember how to access the walkways; I hadn't been on them in years. I was very nervous being jammed in with all those motorists, my body inches from steel bumpers and fenders as I half pedaled, half walked my bike up to a tollbooth. The toll taker working my lane called across to the next booth, "Hey, Mildred, what do we do with bikes?"

Mildred replied, "Let him through. But make sure he doesn't go over the treadle; it'll mess up the count." No one told me where to go after passing through the tollbooth, but I quickly hoisted my bike over the rail and onto the south walkway. I could hardly imagine getting very far on the bridge roadway without being smashed by a motor vehicle—and that was in daylight.[9]

Later, I was to learn that someone in Pearl's position can go into the G.W.B. offices in Fort Lee and request a ride across the bridge. If there's a Port Authority patrolman available, he'll take you across with your bike in his trunk. But none of the bikers I spoke with knew that this service was available or even where the G.W.B. offices are. Pearl certainly didn't. There are also three jitney buses that go from bus stops near the tollbooths in Fort Lee to the bus station, turn around, and come back, though they would not have been available to Pearl that night, given the hour. People from New York who work at the bridge often take these buses.

I asked Pearl if she could sum up what her daily commute by bike across the G.W.B. means to her. "I can in one word," she said. "Freedom."[10]

Some bikers on the walkways are at the start or finish of an expedition. For example, the New York Cycling Club meets in Central Park on Saturdays and Sundays and often pedals up through Manhattan, crosses the George Washington, and then embarks on a round-trip of eighty or a hundred miles, with such destinations as Nyack, New York, or Bear Mountain. There are also charity bikeathons that raise money for worthy causes, such as the annual one for multiple sclerosis that has had as many as 4,500 riders and raised $2.7 million. On the weekend, when traffic is lighter, the cyclists travel through Manhattan, the Lincoln Tunnel (one tube is temporarily closed), and northern New Jersey, returning to Manhattan on a George Washington Bridge walkway.[11]

Pedestrians on the walkways, of course, are there for many different reasons. Some are getting exercise, a few of an extended sort. I met one hiker crossing the bridge who planned, on the New Jersey side, to hike up through Palisades Interstate Park to the New York border, some twelve miles away. "There's a monument there I'd like to see," he said. I've also met New Jersey families with young children who were walking across the bridge with plans to visit the Little Red Lighthouse at the base of the New York tower, the famous book in hand.

I found I was more likely to meet pedestrians who live in Manhattan than in New Jersey. Obviously, Fort Lee is a small city with infinitely fewer potential pedestrians than Manhattan, but there may be another reason. When Jeff Nordstedt of Jersey City worked in Fort Lee in an office overlooking the bridge, it never occurred to him that he might walk over it. "There's that cultural divide between New Jersey and New York," he says. "In New Jersey you drive; in New York you walk. So walking across the bridge into New York just wasn't on my radar screen."[12]

One couple I met on the bridge was from Massachusetts and had come down for a weekend vacation in Manhattan—only they weren't staying in Manhattan. "It's too expensive," they said. "So we're staying in a motel in Fort Lee, where we're parked for free, and walking across the bridge to Manhattan. It's not only saving us a lot of money, but we love the walk, love the adventure." After crossing the bridge, they would get on the subway beneath the bus terminal and head downtown. They had tickets to a Broadway show that evening. I told them that they should be certain to be back on the walkway to New Jersey no later than 11:00 P.M. so they could cross the bridge before the walkway closed at midnight. They had no idea the walkway ever closed. "We might have gotten stranded in Manhattan overnight," they said. "That wouldn't have helped our budget."

Another couple I met lived in Manhattan and was walking to Fort Lee to rent a car and depart on vacation. I asked why this elaborate procedure just to rent a car. "Are you kidding?" the young man asked. "If you rent a car in Manhattan, it can cost you twice what it costs in Jersey. And a cab to Jersey is expensive—you have to pay the driver both ways plus the toll for him to get back to Manhattan plus the tip. So we walk over."

Among the people on the walkway coming from Fort Lee are more than a few Korean Americans. There is a large population of Koreans in Fort Lee: the town is often referred to as "Little Seoul." Once it housed as many as forty-nine tiny movie studios and, from 1903 to the late 1920s, was the center of the American film industry. When moviemaking left for the West Coast, Fort Lee's economy collapsed. The George Washington Bridge revived it, and, more recently, industrious Korean Americans have helped make the town hum with activity.

Washington Heights has a large Latino population, especially Dominicans. On weekdays I've met Dominicans who, in nice weather, walk to jobs in Fort Lee. On a Saturday I met a Dominican from Brooklyn who said that he visits his eighty-three-year-old mother in Washington Heights every week and walks across the bridge with her to New Jersey. They carry food and picnic in Palisades Interstate Park before returning to Manhattan. "Es muy importante para mi madre tomar ejercicio y respirar aire fresco," he told me (Exercise and fresh air are very important for my mother). With the Dominicans on one side of the river and the Koreans on the other, the walkways on the George Washington Bridge have a distinctly ethnic flavor.

Ray Muñoz is a seventy-seven-year-old retired Korean War veteran who lives in Washington Heights. He told me he jogs across the bridge every day, weather permitting, usually returning as a walker. "I have to do it," he said. "I'm a diabetic. The doc says I need exercise. I can't afford a health club, so the bridge is my gym." I asked Ray if he had ever had any unusual experiences crossing the bridge. "Oh, yes," he said. "I'm jogging towards New Jersey, and this guy driving westbound stops his car in the right-hand lane only about thirty or forty yards ahead of me. He doesn't hesitate for a second. He jumps over the railing onto the walkway and then jumps over the outside railing. All of this before I could even shout 'Wait!' I saw his body flip once or twice in the air, but I didn't see him hit the water because of the angle. I ran to the spot and looked below. He was floating facedown. The tide was coming in, and his body was slowly moving upriver. I ran to the New York tower and told the security guard. Later, as I was walking back to Manhattan, I saw the Coast Guard picking him up. I never want to see something like that again."[13]

An African American woman told me she walks on the George Washington Bridge every Saturday "for spiritual reasons." I asked her what she meant. "To contemplate God's glory," she said, her eyes shining. I asked her if she had ever crossed the bridge to New Jersey. "Oh, no," she said, "I go halfway. I just want to be on it. It's my church."

Recently I met a young man on the south walkway who was just standing at the rail about halfway across the bridge looking downriver at the great buildings of Manhattan. He had a CD Walkman sticking out of his pocket and headphones in his ears. When I told him I was writing this book and wanted to talk to him, he removed the headphones.

"You're writing a book on the G.W.B.?" he asked. "That's so cool, especially cool right now."

I asked why it was especially cool right now.

"Because I've come out here on the bridge to say good-bye to New York," he said. "You're writing a book on the bridge and I'm saying good-bye to New York on the bridge." He had been living in Washington

Heights with several other university students, and they had all just graduated. Their apartment was on 178th Street, looking down on the George Washington Bridge Bus Station and out toward the New York tower. "It's been our view for several years now," he said.

His roommates had already left; he was the last. He was flying out of Kennedy Airport later that day, heading for Los Angeles, hoping to break into the film industry. His suitcase was packed and sitting on the floor of the empty apartment. "But I couldn't leave before I came out on the bridge one more time," he said. "This is my bridge."

I told him that a lot of people felt that way.

"But do you know what's the coolest thing of all?" he said. "When you approached I was listening to the Beatles' song 'In My Life.' Do you know how the first line or so of that song goes?"

I confessed that I didn't remember.

"'There are places I'll remember all my life,'" he said. "Here I am on the George Washington Bridge, maybe for the last time in my life, and who do I meet but the guy who's writing the book about the bridge. And when do I meet him? At the exact moment I'm hearing those words, 'There are places I'll remember all my life.' If you had come along a minute or so later, I'd have been gone and we'd never have met. And now you and the song are the sound track of my life."

"I'm honored," I said. "That is cool."

"Way cool," he said. "It's like a novel."

"Maybe," I said, "but if this story was in a novel you'd have to tone it down. Nobody would believe it; it would be too corny."

He looked a little hurt. "But it happened, just like I said."

"Of course," I said. "Coincidences happen all the time in life, but you can't put them in novels. Readers find coincidences contrived. Which is why I'm glad to be writing a nonfiction book this time. I can put this story into the book."

He seemed pleased.

Before we parted, we embraced. We hadn't even exchanged names, but we seemed to mean a lot to each other at that moment. The bridge, like any place of beauty and grandeur, creates an upwelling of affection in people. "Best of luck," I said.

"You too," he replied. He turned and started to walk back to Manhattan.

I turned and started to walk back to New Jersey.

Looking down barrel cables. Courtesy of Dave Frieder.

11

The G. W. B. and Me

I had another opportunity to familiarize myself with the bridge in an uncommon and intimate way on October 26, 2006, the day after the two-day seventy-fifth anniversary festivities for the George Washington Bridge. Even though I had been told that the New York tower is essentially identical to the New Jersey tower, I wanted to experience it anyway; there hadn't been time during my April tour.

I also was keen on examining the New York anchorage to see how it might differ from the New Jersey anchorage, since it is entirely man-made. Late that day, Patrolman Michael Barnable of the Port Authority Police assigned to the George Washington Bridge took me down into it. At several stages of our progress into the giant structure, alarm Klaxons went off and blue lights rotated frantically. Barnable had to call headquarters to explain who we were and what we were doing before he could disable and reset the alarms and we could continue descending down into the very guts of the bridge.

It remains a source of wonder to me how many myths and legends have grown up around the George Washington Bridge. One of them, told to me by several laypeople as if it were a dead certainty, is that the New York anchorage was constructed with contingency plans for the placing of explosives to bring the bridge down if the United States were invaded and the advance of enemy armies had to be stopped at any cost. This, like the myth about the bodies in the concrete, is simply untrue. Still, however silly these stories may be, they do add to the bridge's mystique.

Once you're inside, the concrete New York anchorage is essentially identical to its New Jersey counterpart built into Palisades rock. It has a north and a south side, with two barrel cables entering each. All four cables splay out into sixty-one three-inch strands of wire, each wrapping around a chain of massive eye-bars sunk into the concrete. Barnable showed me the catwalk from which a worker in the anchorage had recently fallen to his death. The catwalk had no outside railing. It does now.

Inspector Larry Fields, who is in charge of security at the George Washington Bridge and commands the eighty-five Port Authority policemen there, had arranged for me to go down into the anchorage. The silver-haired Fields is articulate and smart and is known as a cop's cop. He is famous in Port Authority Police circles for once rappelling down the inside of a dark elevator shaft in the World Trade Center, where he was chief of security from 1996 to 1998.[1]

Photograph taken in 1931 inside the mostly complete New York anchorage, into which Patrolman Michael Barnable led the author on October 26, 2006. The stringers hanging from the barrel cables await a final section of roadway.

For some months Fields had also said he would arrange the visit to the New York tower for me but had to coordinate with "the E.S.U. police." Not wanting to betray my ignorance, I didn't ask what "E.S.U." stands for. Nor did I understand that the E.S.U. police—not normally assigned to the George Washington Bridge—were not under Fields's direct supervision. Finally, after several delays, the date was set.

When I arrived at the bridge offices at 220 Bruce Reynolds Boulevard that morning, I was surprised to encounter four officers in special gear waiting for me. "Let's go," Lieutenant Richard Munnelly said, and the five of us went outside and got into two of the special vehicles the E.S.U. (Emergency Services Unit, I now learned) employs. These were more like Humvees than patrol cars, and inside each were heavy weapons. These men were not like other Port Authority Police. They were more akin to Army Rangers or Navy SEALs. The eighty E.S.U. police are stationed in Journal Square in Jersey City, ready to respond to any dire emergency or terrorist attack. They also help provide security for the president of the United States when he comes to the Greater New York area. I kept wondering why four of these gentlemen were required to go along with me. All I needed, I had figured, was one ordinary patrolman to go up with me in the elevators, not four guys who looked like a SWAT team.

We drove out onto the bridge heading east and, turning around at one of the places only available to official cars, pulled up on hash marks next to where the north barrel cables were passing through the roadway en route to the New York anchorage. I had thought we would pull up by the tower, where the elevator is. Before I could say anything, Sergeant Kevin Cottrell was outfitting me. "Step into this harness," he said, "like putting on a pair of pants." I wondered what the harness was for. "Okay," he said, "now let's slip the other harness over your head." He did so, and then, after a good deal of belt adjusting, snap fastening, and Velcro engaging, the two harnesses were as one. A large U-shaped hook protruded from the spot where they joined, and from it ropes with brass fasteners played out to the right and to the left. "Hold on to these fasteners," Cottrell said. Then he plunked a hard hat on my head and adjusted the chin strap. I put on the pair of gloves he handed me. What was all this? I certainly hadn't needed any of this equipment when I went up in the New Jersey tower elevators with Bob Durando and Bob McKee. Weren't these guys being overly cautious?

"Okay," Cottrell said, "let's go. Patrolmen Jerry Fredella and Mark Legiec will lead. You'll be in the middle and I'll be immediately behind you. The lieutenant will bring up the rear. Any questions?"

"Uh, yeah," I said. "Where are we going?"

"Didn't you want to go up?" Cottrell asked, pointing to the top of the tower.

"Uh. . . . yeah," I repeated, adding, under my breath, "but. . . ." It had suddenly dawned on me what Cottrell had in mind. We weren't going up in elevators. These guys planned for us to climb a barrel cable to the very top of the tower. I couldn't quite bring myself to say what I was really thinking, which was, to be perfectly plain about it, "Ohhhh shit!" But I couldn't quite back out, either. Besides, I had my Appalachian Mountain Club cap on under my hard hat. A regular hiker and mountain climber, I would handle this somehow, I told myself. And told myself again.

In a moment the gate of the enclosure surrounding the barrel cables had been opened and, bracketed by my companions, I mounted the inside barrel cable, Cable C. The two cables on the south side of the bridge are A and B; the two on the north side are C and D. The outside cables, A and D, hold the emerald lights. D was nine feet away from C, center to center. I wondered if anyone had ever tried to leap from one cable to the other. Not a good idea, I was sure. I was instructed to snap my brass fasteners onto the seven-eighths-inch "hand ropes," guide cables that run along each side of the barrel cables waist high.

We began climbing the barrel cable, our gloved hands pushing the brass fasteners in front of us on the hand ropes. I decided that if these guys were prepared to take me up there I probably wouldn't die—unless it was of fright.

In addition to all the other challenges, we were walking on a rounded surface, so I had to place my feet carefully. And who were these guys kidding with the hard hats? Suicides die when they jump from the Upper Level and fall only some 225 feet to the river. We were climbing to something like 375 feet above the road surface, 604 feet above the rocks of Jeffrey's Hook on which the New York tower stands. It was good I didn't know in advance what had been planned for me by Inspector Fields and these E.S.U. guys. I wouldn't have done it for a million bucks. Or, perhaps more likely, I'd have had a nervous-breakdown-sized bout of indecision.

The kindly Cottrell seemed to sense my fear. "Mind over matter," he said quietly from his position behind me. "Mind over matter. If you find yourself freaking out, just say so and we won't continue." I thought about not continuing, but this would have entailed unhooking and turning around, which seemed almost as scary as just continuing up the barrel cable. Also, I was damned if I would freak out. "Compartmentalize," I kept saying to myself. "Compartmentalize. What's the worst that can happen? Okay, I die. But if I don't die, this'll be great material for the book."

A short way along the barrel cable, we reached the first pair of steel stanchions that hold up the hand ropes. Every fifty feet there are such stanchions. Cottrell told me that if a climber ever slipped, the farthest he could slide down the barrel would be fifty feet before his brass fasteners hit the first stanchions below and he was abruptly halted. Yeah, *only* fifty feet, I thought. What fun that would be, sliding fifty feet on your backside on a cable hundreds of feet up in the air. And you'd probably slide the whole fifty because these stanchion points are the likeliest places to slip. At the stanchions, two suspender cables, or stringers, loop over the barrel cables and are bolted inside "cable bands"—sleeves that are attached to the barrels—so you're walking on a surface that's not only round but bumpy. I was glad it wasn't raining that day, making the surface also slippery. The wind was blowing strongly, though. At such a height there is nothing to stop the wind that sweeps down the Hudson.

But what makes the stanchions especially scary places is that you have to open the brass fasteners there and reattach them to the hand ropes just beyond the stanchions. "One at a time," Cottrell cautioned. Still, every time I unhooked I would, for some seconds, be attached to the guide cables by only one rope. I wondered what it would be like to dangle below the barrel cable by one rope, whether it would support my weight and, if so, how anyone could pull me back onto the cable. As an extra precaution, I was tethered to Patrolman Legiec immediately in front of me. At first I found this comforting. But then I began to think: what if Legiec, who was much bigger than me, slipped and slid backward, knocking my feet out from under me?

The barrel cables rise at a precipitous angle, reaching forty-four degrees as you approach the top. That's just shy of halfway to straight up. You have the sensation of climbing straight up into the sky—like Jack in the "Jack and the Beanstalk" story, with the tower ahead faintly representing the giant. Because of the extreme angle, Legiec, who preceded me by only a few feet, was always substantially higher, increasing my sense of his size and what the impact might be if he slipped. I didn't like this being tethered at all.

I also kept wondering why Fredella, who was the youngest of the group and our point man, had the nickname "Devil." "Why's he called that?" I grunted to Cottrell over my shoulder.

"Just what we call him," he replied, which didn't reassure me. I hoped Devil wasn't the kind of guy who took unnecessary risks. Things were already plenty risky for me.

As I climbed, I began to have a new fear. What if I got a cramp in a calf muscle? How could I possibly get rid of it up here? And the climbing was all in the calves. I knew that because mine were turning into rocks inside my jeans.

From time to time Cottrell would ask, "You all right?"

"Sure," I would tell him. I wasn't going to say otherwise. I knew that if I ever talked about how scared I was, it would only make me more scared. I just kept my eyes glued in front of me on Legiec's boots. I didn't want to look up to where the giant tower beckoned, except to occasionally ascertain that it was getting closer, and I certainly didn't want to look down.

The climb, one step at a time, was a metaphor for a lot of things: for building a house board by board; for writing a book word by word—plus terror, of course. The only terror in writing a book is facing an empty white page. I was still telling myself: "Compartmentalize." I thought of Zen. I thought of "Be here now." I told myself that the climb was a kind of meditation. I just had to stay in my zone, be here now.

Slowly, we advanced toward the top. The wind was blowing a gale up there, and I worried about being literally blown off the barrel cable. Also, though this hadn't been a particularly cold day down below, up here the wind chill was fierce. I hadn't dressed appropriately for the occasion. I thought about hypothermia. I thought about the man found high up in one of the towers some years ago, frozen to death, like one of those bodies occasionally found up in the Himalayas. It was never discovered why he climbed up there. Some believe he was intent on suicide, changed his mind, but couldn't get down and died of the cold.

Now we were approaching the top, and the angle of the barrel cable was so steep my head was leaning back, my feet well forward of my head. Patrolman Fredella moved forward and, climbing onto a little steel platform attached to the tower, worked the handle of the door leading into the saddle room. It didn't budge. He tried it again. I couldn't believe it: it was locked from the inside. I had made it to fifteen feet from the top and now I was stuck. Lieutenant Munnelly got out his radio, and over the squawking coming from the other end I heard him say, "You gotta be kidding." Then he shouted to me over the wind, "Don't worry, they're coming. They'll be up here in fifteen minutes."

Fifteen minutes?! Did I really have to stand there on the barrel cable for fifteen extra minutes with the wind howling and just wait? I stole tiny looks below, the first time I had looked down during the whole forty minutes of climbing the barrel. Everything was tiny except for the giant tower in front of us that I could almost touch. There was a loud sound, and it was coming closer. A blue helicopter with PORT AUTHORITY written on its side circled us, and I could see the pilot clearly. Did he intend to strafe us? "What's he doing?" I asked Cottrell.

"Probably checking on us," he said.

"Why?" I asked.

Cottrell shrugged. The helicopter wheeled off toward the south.

This seemed a good time for a photo. Taking pictures would pass the time and take my mind off our ridiculous position on the barrel cable. I wanted a picture to prove to my family that I'd been up here. Heck, I wanted a picture to prove to myself that I'd been up here. I handed Legiec a disposable camera I was carrying in my jacket pocket, and, untethering from me, he climbed up onto the platform next to Fredella. The two of them took turns snapping pictures with Cottrell and Munnelly behind me, and behind them the bridge deck far below and all of Manhattan beyond it.

What seemed like ages later, there was a scraping sound inside the saddle room and the door opened. A patrolman had driven out onto the bridge from the G.W.B. offices, turned around in Manhattan, parked by the New York tower, and come up the elevators to the saddle room. Fredella and Legiec went inside. There was a tricky moment when I had to unfasten myself from the guide cables altogether to get into the room, when momentarily I wasn't attached to anything. Then, followed by Cottrell and Munnelly I scrambled inside.

I was suffused with a feeling of deep satisfaction. If I were on Bob McKee's staff, I would probably now be "height certified." Like David Copperfield, we all want to be the heroes of our own lives, and, at a somewhat advanced age, I had just done the bravest thing in mine. I would never climb Mount Everest, but, after admiring the George Washington Bridge's towers all my life, I had just scaled one of them— something I could never have imagined doing as a boy when my friends and I would walk over the bridge to New Jersey. Then it was only the bridge. Now it was also my bridge. I had taken possession of it; I was ready to write this book.

Photo of the author scaling barrel cable C toward the New York tower with Sergeant Kevin Cottrell and Lieutenant Richard Munnelly of the Emergency Service Unit Police immediately behind him.

Acknowledgments

S o many people and institutions helped me write this book that I feel a bit guilty thanking them here at the back, but there were my readers to consider as well: I wanted to get them onto the bridge as quickly as possible. Also, readers tend to skip over acknowledgments when they appear at the beginning. Perhaps now, those who have enjoyed the book may wish to look through these acknowledgments just as those who take film seriously as an art form sit through the credits at the end of a movie as a form of homage to those who contributed to it and as a way of finding out who did what. I should add that all those acknowledged as associated with various institutions are listed with the positions they occupied when I conducted my research.

I would first like to thank Dr. Margot Ammann Durrer, daughter of Othmar Ammann, who, from the start, has supported my efforts with stories, documents, and good cheer. She helped me to understand her father's accomplishments and the kind of man he was. Without her help I could not have begun to bring his wonderful story to life on the printed page.

George Washington Bridge staff were always generous with their time and with helping me dig out facts and the sources of anecdotes. Robert Durando, presently general manager of the bridge, and Robert McKee, physical plant manager, were always the go-to guys who would get me what I needed to know, or at least tell me who could do so. I have bugged them nonstop for two years now, and they've never complained. Other key people at the bridge were Olga Krueger, supervisor of bridge operations, and Andrea Giorgi Bocker, chief resident engineer.

Without the help and support of Inspector Larry Fields of the Port Authority Police, chief of bridge security, I would not have come to know and, more important, intimately experience the bridge. I am especially grateful to Fields for assigning Port Authority patrolmen to accompany me on my adventures and grateful as well to Patrolman Michael Barnable and Emergency Service Unit Police Lieutenant Richard Munnelly, Sergeant Kevin Cottrell, and Patrolmen Jerry Fredella and Mark Legiec. Although he was not assigned to the bridge per se, I also wish to especially thank Port Authority Patrolman Michael Teel for orienting me to the bridge and the means by which I might gain access to its top staff and, through them, its facilities.

Former staff at the George Washington Bridge were often as helpful as present staff, perhaps because they missed the bridge so much they had an even greater need to talk about it than those now working there. Jerry Del Tufo, former physical plant manager at the G.W.B. and now general manager of the three Port Authority Staten Island bridges, helped me in every way possible—not only with his time but by providing key documents and several of the photographs in this book. Kenneth Philmus, now retired from the Port Authority but formerly general manager of the G.W.B. and later director of the Division of Tunnels, Bridges, and Terminals, and Robert Eadicicco, former supervisor of bridge operations and now general manager of the Holland Tunnel, were also very important to my efforts. I also wish to thank John Teel, formerly an electrician at the bridge, for his wonderful stories and keen insight, as well as for sharing various bridge memorabilia with me.

At the Port Authority Offices in Manhattan, Steve Napolitano, now assistant director of the Division of Tunnels, Bridges, and Terminals and former general manager of the George Washington Bridge, was immensely helpful. So was the current director of that department, Victoria Kelly. Another person at Port Authority headquarters I must thank is Tiffany Townsend of the Public Affairs Department, who went out of her way to help me gain access to people, documents, and pictures. Shawn Laurenti, director of government and community relations, was also helpful and supportive.

Dave Frieder, nicknamed "the Bridge Man" because of his daring exploits in photographing bridges high in the sky, generously shared his immense knowledge of the G.W.B., as well as his incredible collection of bridge artifacts. Three other artists fascinated by the George Washington Bridge were inspiring to me: Faith Ringgold, Valeri Larko, and Steven Siegel. I hope my verbal imagery does justice to their visual imagery.

A number of individuals associated with a variety of institutions went out of their way to be helpful: David Shayt, engineering curator at the National Museum of American History; Ron Becker and Fernanda Perrone, of Special Collections and University Archives at the Rutgers University libraries; Jean Lee Poggi, coordinator of the West 181st Street Beautification Project; Bill Lieberman, of Bauer Publishing; Ourida Oubriham, deputy director of the library at the Stevens Institute of Technology; Lucille Bertram, of the Fort Lee Historical Society; Jennifer Coultas, of the Boonton Historical Society and Museum; Chris Jochim, Ann McDade, Heidi Schwab, and Polly Lacey, of the Morristown and Morris Township Public Library; Carol Reese, of the American Society of Civil Engineers; the staff of the New-York Historical Society; Kevin Collins, vice chair of the Palisades Interstate Park Commission, and Jim Hall, executive director of Palisades Interstate Park; Edward Laing, of the Ammann and Whitney engineering firm; Kristen Nitray, special collections archivist at Stony Brook University; and Leslie Feder, of Feder and Stia Architects.

Several people in the academic world were helpful in different ways in shaping this book. They include Steven Lubar, director of the John Nicholas Brown Center for the Study of American Civilization at Brown University; Alan Trachtenberg, professor emeritus at Yale University; Richard Haw, of the John Jay College of Criminal Justice; and Nell Dillon-Emers, of Columbia University. Finally, colleagues in the Rutgers University American Studies Department early on permitted me to present my ideas for this book in a symposium format and gave me much good advice on how to proceed. Angus Kress Gillespie, Helene Grynberg, Nicole Fleetwood, and Louise Barnett were especially helpful.

At Rutgers University Press, Marlie Wasserman, director, Marilyn Campbell, prepress director, Christina Brianik, assistant to the director, and India Cooper, copy editor, were always encouraging and helpful with advice on how to make this book not just informative but fun. If this book is attractive, both verbally and visually, much of the credit is due them.

A number of my present and former students helped with research. Principal among them were Alex Rabinowitz and Jessica Schneider. Others who helped were Maggie De Menna, Hana Wilenchik, Janelle Gendrano, and Garret Broad. A former student, Dr. Lisa P. Davidson, pointed me to George Washington Bridge artifacts in the collection of the National Museum of American History.

Others, not students, were helpful to my research, especially Carole Goldstein, who displayed genius in finding materials unavailable to someone with other than superb computer skills. Eddie Konczal, with Computer Services at Rutgers University, was, as always, remarkably supportive of my needs and patient with my technical backwardness.

Family members, including Kate Rockland, David Rockland, Joshua Rockland, Alana Rockland, Sarah Dutton, John Anglim, and Barbara Rubin, helped me in significant ways.

Special thanks are due my wife, Patricia Ard, whose rigorous and perceptive reading of chapter drafts and enthusiastic support for this book from its inception were essential to whatever success it may have as literature.

Finally, gratitude is due the Eastern Frontier Educational Foundation for its invitation to spend several weeks during the summer of 2007 in residence on Norton Island off the coast of Maine. There, with the aid of absolute seclusion by day, good fellowship with other writers by night, and considerable distance from the George Washington Bridge so as to see it afresh, I had the perfect support system to finish the book's penultimate draft.

I hope everyone thanked in these acknowledgments will take pleasure in this book.

Notes

Introduction

1. E-mail from Margot Ammann Durrer, May 30, 2007. I am grateful to Dave Frieder for pointing me to the story about Ammann and the Erector Set. Frieder, a celebrated photographer of bridges, possesses a veritable museum of George Washington Bridge artifacts, including five Erector Sets in mint condition that he stores under his bed. Erector Sets were popular toys manufactured by the A. C. Gilbert Co. of New Haven, Connecticut, from 1911 to 1967. I interviewed Frieder at his home in New Milford, New Jersey, on April 1, 2006.
2. Shayt is an associate curator in the Division of Work and Industry. He made the remark in a telephone conversation with me on June 4, 2006.
3. Address of Franklin Roosevelt, *George Washington Bridge over the Hudson River Between New York and New Jersey, Addresses Delivered October 24, 1931*, published by the Port of New York Authority.
4. Directed by Frank Capra, RKO Radio Pictures, 1946.
5. John Teel, interview, December 4, 2005.
6. Rogers, America's favorite humorist, and Post, an aviation pioneer, were killed when their biplane crashed in 1935 en route to the Orient at Point Barrow, Alaska, now the northernmost point in the United States.
7. For the seventy-fifth anniversary of the bridge in 2006, the Port Authority issued a small picture book titled *George Washington Bridge: A Timeless Marvel*, edited by Darl Rastorfer.
8. Written and directed by Martin Bruch, Satel Films, 2003.
9. Ken Philmus, interview, June 14, 2006.

Chapter 1. A Day on the G.W.B.

1. E-mail from Bob McKee, June 29, 2007. Throughout this chapter, and throughout the book, I mention many exchanges with Bob Durando and Bob McKee. These took place on the bridge, in their offices, on the telephone, and through many e-mails.
2. Steve Napolitano, interview, May 24, 2006.
3. Ken Philmus, interview, June 14, 2006.
4. Jerry Del Tufo, interview, April 17, 2006.
5. These figures are based on the number of tolls collected at the bridge of vehicles traveling eastbound. The G.W.B. authorities double the figures on the assumption that surely as many vehicles cross the bridge westbound as eastbound, which may be a conservative estimate, since no tolls are collected in that direction and there are people who will do anything to avoid a toll.
6. Michelangelo Conte, "Pulaski Skyway Replacement Being Designed," *Star-Ledger,* February 12, 2007, 13. Patrick McGeehan, "A Bridge That Has Nowhere to Go: The Tappan Zee Turns 50, a Risky Age for Its Kind," *New York Times,* January 17, 2006, B-1. On the Minneapolis bridge, see "A Bridge in America Just Shouldn't Fall Down," editorial, *USA Today,* August 3, 2007, 10A; and "A Bridge Collapses," editorial, *New York Times,* August 5, 2007, sec. 4, 9. "One out of five" is from the dust jacket of Henry Petroski, *Engineers of Dreams: Great Bridge Builders and the Spanning of America* (New York: Knopf, 1995).
7. Laurie Johnston, "Child Friends of Small Lighthouse Shocked by News It's Up for Sale," *New York Times,* July 11, 1951, 2.
8. "There Grew a Little Flower." *Ruddigore* was first performed in 1887.

Chapter 2. The George and the Brooklyn:
New Jersey and New York

1. Hendrik Hertzberg, "Gorgeous George," *New Yorker,* March 26, 2001, 76.
2. I am grateful to Richard Haw for pointing to this disconnect in his book *Brooklyn Bridge: A Cultural History* (New Brunswick: Rutgers University Press, 2005), 7–13.
3. Peter Quinn, "Bridge Builder," *American Heritage* 53, no. 5 (October 2002), 40.
4. Darl Rastorfer, *Six Bridges: The Legacy of Othmar Ammann* (New Haven: Yale University Press, 2000), ix.

5. Margot Ammann Durrer, interview, January 26, 2007.

6. Le Corbusier (Charles Edouard Jeanneret-Gris), *When the Cathedrals Were White* (New York: McGraw-Hill, 1947), 77.

7. David Steinman, *Bridges and Their Builders* (New York: G. P. Putnam's Sons, 1941), 340.

8. Paul Goldberger, *The City Observed, New York: A Guide to the Architecture of Manhattan* (New York: Random House, 1979), 324.

9. There is a little suspension bridge over a creek that courses through the Douglass campus of Rutgers University, where I teach—built with Roebling wire, I might add. The bridge is nicknamed "Old Bouncer" because it moves up and down a great deal even when only one person is crossing it. It parallels another bridge with steel support descending to the ravine banks below. Not long ago I found myself by the suspension bridge responding to a first-year student who wanted to know, "What holds it up?" Even after I explained she said, "I think I'll take the other one." Since suspension bridges are flexible, there is an inherent suspicion of them, even though their safety record is the equal of any other bridge. However, some years before I approached the bridge just after a large number of people, exiting a campus meeting, had crossed it. To my horror, I discovered that several of the stiff vertical suspenders attached to its cables had snapped. I cordoned off the bridge and called the campus police. I learned that day the superiority of spun cables over forged iron supports.

10. Goldberger, *City Observed*, 325.

11. Martin Kushner, interview, December 6, 2006.

12. The symposium "American Icons" was sponsored by Columbia's American Studies Program and took place on March 4, 1987.

13. Alice Caulkins, interview, December 16, 2006.

14. Saul Steinberg, "View of the World from 9th Avenue," *New Yorker*, March 29, 1976, cover. The Alan Dunn cartoon is reproduced in *The Complete Cartoons of the New Yorker*, ed. Robert Mankoff (New York: Black Dog & Leventhal Publishers, 2004), 41. Bruce McCall, "Op-Art," *New York Times*, July 2, 2006, sec. 4, 11. Robert Strauss, telephone interview, April 27, 2006.

15. Written by Woody Allen and Marshall Brickman, directed by Woody Allen, United Artists, 1973.

16. See Michael Aaron Rockland, "For Ellis Island, a New Life," *New Jersey Monthly*, July 2000, 48–51, 66–67.

17. Jameson Doig, *Empire on the Hudson* (New York: Columbia University Press, 2001), 402.

18. Today there is concern that the Port Authority, with its own policing and bond-issuing powers, has become something of a third state. See the editorial "The Port Authority Shuts Out the Public," *Star-Ledger,* October 16, 2006, 14.

19. Ron Marisco, "Gray and Beautiful at 75: A Depression-Era Wonder Marks Milestone Wednesday," *Star-Ledger,* October 23, 2006, 1, 6. "G W B 75," *Record,* October 22, 2006, sec. Z, 1–12. The building of the G.W.B. did lead to massive development in New Jersey, just as the building of the Brooklyn Bridge led to massive development in Brooklyn. Soon Bergen, mostly rural, became New Jersey's most populous county, just as Brooklyn became the most populous of New York's boroughs. Accelerated growth, to the considerable betterment of many New Yorkers, had been predicted by New Jersey governor Morgan Larson at the inauguration of the bridge on October 24, 1931: "The verdant hills and valleys of North Jersey will prove a veritable paradise to hundreds of families who have heretofore been compelled to live in cramped quarters." And a New Jersey publication at that time asserted that, because of the bridge, New Jersey "was at the threshold of its greatest era" (*Jersey Observer,* published in Hoboken, November 1931, 1).

20. Pete Donohue, "Spanning the Ages: 75 Years!" *Daily News,* October 25, 2006, 27.

21. Alan Trachtenberg, telephone interview, November 15, 2005. Trachtenberg's book is *Brooklyn Bridge: Fact and Symbol* (New York: Oxford University Press, 1965).

22. Quoted in Edward Cohen et al., "The Engineer and His Works: A Tribute to Othmar Hermann Ammann," *Annals of the New York Academy of Sciences* 136, no. 23 (1966), 729.

23. Philip Lopate, *Waterfront: A Journey Around Manhattan* (New York: Crown, 2004), 266. Montgomery Schuyler, "The Bridge as a Monument," *Harper's Weekly,* May 26, 1883, 326.

24. Lopate, *Waterfront,* 179.

25. James Morris, *The Great Port: A Passage Through New York* (New York: Harcourt Brace, 1969), 156.

26. Letter from Richard Haw, December 2, 2005.

27. Arline Dodge, interview, December 19, 2006.

28. Camille Paglia, 1990, quoted in "I: On Infrastructure, Gender," www.nypl.org/admin/exhibitions/ioni/genderi.

Chapter 3. Othmar Ammann

1. Quoted in Henry Petroski, *Engineers of Dreams: Great Bridge Builders and the Spanning of America* (New York: Knopf, 1995), 281.

2. David P. Billington in the film "Bridging New York," part of the P.B.S. *Great Projects: The Building of America* series, written and produced by Daniel A. Miller, 2002. For the best discussion of Ammann's technical and aesthetic achievements overall, see Darl Rastorfer, *Six Bridges: The Legacy of Othmar H. Ammann* (New Haven: Yale University Press, 2000).

3. Letter, December 12, 1927, provided and translated by Margot Ammann Durrer.

4. Quoted in M. K. Wisehart, "The Greatest Bridge in the World and the Man Who Is Building It," *American Magazine*, no. 34 (June 1928), 183.

5. From an unpublished Othmar Ammann scrapbook compiled by Margot Ammann Durrer.

6. Quoted in Petroski, *Engineers of Dreams*, 210.

7. Letter to Lilly Wehrli, May 11, 1904, provided and translated by Margot Ammann Durrer.

8. Urs C. Widmer, "Othmar Hermann Ammann, 1879–1965: His Way to Great Bridges," *Swiss American Historical Society Newsletter* 15 (1979), 5, 6.

9. It is often stated incorrectly that when the George Washington was built, the suspended span between towers was exactly twice the length of the next largest suspension bridge. Such commentators have in mind the 1,750-foot suspended length of the Delaware River Bridge, now known as the Ben Franklin Bridge, from Camden, New Jersey, to Philadelphia. However, another, slightly longer bridge with a suspended span of 1,850 feet was completed before the G.W.B., the Ambassador Bridge over the Detroit River to Canada.

10. Quoted in James Tobin, *Great Projects* (New York: Free Press, 2001), 194, 195.

11. Letter to his mother, April 21, 1921, provided and translated by Margot Amman Durrer.

12. *Technology Review* 33, no. 9 (July 1931), reprinted in Smithsonian Institution, *Annual Report, 1931.*

13. Othmar Ammann, "General Conception and Development of Design," *George Washington Bridge Across the Hudson River at New York, N.Y.* (New York: American Society of Civil Engineers in Collaboration with the Port of New York Authority), *Transactions of the A.S.C.E.* 97, no. 1818 (1933), 2.

14. Entry of March 22, 1923. I am grateful to Margot Ammann Durrer for providing me with a photocopy of this text in Ammann's handwriting. Ammann's daybooks are now kept in the Ammann Archive in his alma mater, the Polytechnic Institute in Zurich.

15. Letter to his mother, December 14, 1923, provided and translated by Margot Ammann Durrer.

16. Ibid.

17. Ayn Rand, *The Fountainhead* (New York: Bobbs-Merrill, 1943).

18. Margot Ammann Durrer, "Memories of My Father," *Swiss American Historical Review,* April 4, 1979, 6, 7.

19. Quoted in Petroski, *Engineers of Dreams,* 253.

20. Silzer to Cohen, May 22, 1924. See Jameson Doig, "Politics and the Engineering Mind: O. H. Ammann and the Hidden Story of the George Washington Bridge," *Yearbook of German-American Relations* 25 (1990), 172.

21. David Luberoff, "Learning from Ammann," *Architecture Boston* (July/August 2004), 27.

22. Letter, December 20, 1923. The actual letter is reproduced in Doig, "Politics and the Engineering Mind," 188.

23. Letter, February 14, 1924, translated by Margot Ammann Durrer.

24. Milton MacKaye, "Poet in Steel," *New Yorker,* June 2, 1934, 32.

25. Letter, September 12, 1926, provided and translated by Margot Ammann Durrer.

26. Letter from Rosa Labhardt Ammann, March 14, 1926, translated by Margot Ammann Durrer.

27. E-mail from Margot Ammann Durrer, October 16, 2007.

28. From the Othmar Ammann scrapbook, courtesy of Margot Ammann Durrer.

29. Ammann Durrer, "Memories of My Father," 6, 7.

30. Ibid.

31. From the Othmar Ammann scrapbook, courtesy of Margot Ammann Durrer.

32. Translation by Margot Amman Durrer from Widmer, "Othmar Hermann Ammann, 1879–1965," 6.

33. For example, the Holland Tunnel, inaugurated in 1927, was completed in twice its projected time and at four times the projected cost.

34. MacKaye, "Poet in Steel," 32.

35. See Petroski, *Engineers of Dreams,* 288.

36. Edward Laing, telephone interviews, January 15 and June 20, 2007.

37. Quoted in Gay Talese, *The Bridge* (New York: Harper & Row, 1964), 31.

38. Ibid., 46.

39. Quoted in Petroski, *Engineers of Dreams*, 318.

40. Ibid.

41. E-mail from Margot Ammann Durrer, June 4, 2007. The commentator is Gay Talese in the film "Bridging New York," part of the P.B.S. *Great Projects: The Building of America* series, written and produced by Daniel A. Miller, 2002.

42. Margot Ammann Durrer, interviews, January 25, 2006, and January 26, 2007.

Chapter 4. Building the Bridge

1. Indeed, Ammann's own Bayonnne or Kill Van Kull, an arch bridge, may soon have to be replaced because, by 2007, some of the giant new container ships heading for Port Elizabeth were forced to pass under it gingerly, with only ten feet of clearance.

2. Carolyn Marshall, "U.S. Prosecutors Start Investigating Oil Spill," *New York Times*, November 13, 2007, A-25.

3. Othmar Ammann, "Brobdingnagian Bridges," *Technology Review* 33, no. 9 (July 1931), republished in the *Smithsonian Annual Report* for 1931.

4. Harold Ross, Talk of the Town, "Big Bridge," *New Yorker*, December 22, 1934, 10.

5. Letter to Emilie Rosa Labhardt Ammann, December 12, 1927, provided and translated by Margot Ammann Durrer.

6. William Meredith, "The Cemetery Bridge," *Poems Are Hard to Read* (Ann Arbor: University of Michigan Press, 1990), 55, 56.

7. E-mail from Bob Durando, November 6, 2006. Mary Ellen Schoonmaker, "Daring Young Men and Their Sky-High Jobs," *Bergen Record*, October 18, 1981, A-5.

8. Ammann was named head of a team, called for by Congress, to look into exactly why this bridge, located some thirty miles south of Seattle and nicknamed "Galloping Gertie"—because of its extreme oscillations even while under construction—came down. Afterward, at Robert Moses's insistence, but with mixed feelings, he put stiffening trusses on one of his own bridges, the Bronx-Whitestone, which had been completed in a fashion not dissimilar to the Tacoma Narrows Bridge just the year before. The amateur film footage of the Tacoma Narrows Bridge self-destructing is shown around the world in engineering classes, in which every frame is carefully examined in a manner not unlike the way the Zapruder film of the assassination of President John F. Kennedy is gone over by conspiracy theorists.

9. "World's Greatest Bridge Links Two States," *New York Times*, October 18, 1934, 1. Valerie Jablow, "Othmar Ammann's Glory," *Smithsonian* 30, no. 7 (October 1999), 36.

Chapter 5. The Accidental Icon

1. Bob McKee, telephone interview, March 20, 2007.
2. Leon Moisseiff, "George Washington Bridge: Design of the Towers," *Transactions of the American Society of Civil Engineers* 97, no. 1821 (1933), 165.
3. Alan Trachtenberg, *Brooklyn Bridge: Fact and Symbol* (New York: Oxford University Press, 1965), 80.
4. Quoted in David P. Billington, *The Tower and the Bridge: The New Art of Structural Engineering* (New York: Basic Books, 1983), 143.
5. Othmar Ammann, "General Conception and Development of Design," *George Washington Bridge Across the Hudson River at New York, N.Y.* (New York: American Society of Civil Engineers in Collaboration with the Port of New York Authority), *Transactions of the A.S.C.E.* 97, no. 1818 (1933), 251.
6. Margot Ammann Durrer, interview, November 24, 2006.
7. Ammann, "General Conception," 234, 51.
8. Ibid., 51. C. T. Schwartz, "Discussion on the Eight Papers," *Transactions of the American Society of Civil Engineers* 97, no. 1826 (1933), 422.
9. Margot Ammann Durrer, interview, November 24, 2006.
10. In recent years, cable-stayed bridges have increasingly been in vogue. These have no barrel cables or anchorages. Multiple suspender-like cables are played out directly from one or both sides of whatever towers are erected to all points on the suspended portions of such bridges. The roadways thus hang directly from the towers.
11. John Kouwenhoven, *The Arts in Modern American Civilization* (New York: W. W. Norton, 1948), 206. "The Skyline: Bridges and Buildings," *New Yorker*, November 12, 1931, 12.
12. Quoted in Herbert Muschamp, "For Rebuilders, Inspiration All Around," *New York Times*, October 5, 2001, E-27. "Mr. Ammann's Work of Art," *New York Times*, August 20, 1962, 23.
13. S. J. Woolf, "A Master Builder Looks Ahead," *New York Times Magazine*, April 15, 1934, 7.
14. Le Corbusier (Charles Edouard Jeanneret-Gris), *When the Cathedrals Were White* (New York: McGraw-Hill, 1947), 75, 76.

15. Darl Rastorfer, *Six Bridges: The Legacy of Othmar H. Ammann* (New Haven: Yale University Press, 2000), 45.

16. Moisseiff, "George Washington Bridge: Design of the Towers," 165.

17. Goldberger, *City Observed*, 325. Goldberger went on to say, "To stand underneath the gray steel towers, looking straight up at the web of metalwork . . . is to celebrate structure as you can nowhere in New York. You feel the soaring cables, their curving lines sharp against the sky; they move and push, and the structure holds, frames, enforces. The towers are the rational conscience, the cables the romantic impulse, and together they make harmony" (326).

18. Quoted in Alden Whitman, "Expressed Industrial Spirit," *New York Times*, August 19, 1969, 28.

19. Ibid. This statement is Whitman's own.

20. Kouwenhoven, *Arts in Modern American Civilization*, 204–206.

21. Othmar Amman, "The Hell Gate Arch Bridge and Approaches of the New York Connecting Railroad over the East River in New York City," *Transactions of the American Society of Civil Engineers* 82 (December 1918), 986. Amman's views were seconded by the consulting architect on his Bronx-Whitestone Bridge, completed in 1939 just in time for the World's Fair. Said Aymar Embury II, "Engineers should be good architects and architects good engineers." Quoted in Petroski, *Engineers of Dreams*, 291.

22. "The Skyline: Bridges and Buildings," *New Yorker*, November 21, 1931, 12.

23. Petroski, *Engineers of Dreams*, jacket copy.

24. Frank D. Welch, *Philip Johnson and Texas* (Austin: University of Texas, 2000), 318. Robert Campbell, "This May Be the Year of Wright," *Boston Globe*, January 23, 1990. David Billington makes a similar point in his book *The Tower and the Bridge: The New Art of Structural Engineering* (New York: Basic Books, 1983), when he writes, "It is as crucial for engineers to learn about art and aesthetics as it is for artists to learn about structure and construction" (xvi).

25. Letter from Leslie Feder, July 30, 2006. Feder is with Feder and Stia Architects LLP.

26. This statement is often incorrectly attributed to Marcel Duchamp himself. As recently as the 2006 Whitney Museum retrospective, entitled "Full House," Duchamp is credited with this remark. However, in the exhibit "Steiglitz and His Circle," in the Museo Reina Sofia in Madrid in 2005, the statement is reproduced in the journal *Blind Man*, nos. 1 and 2 (April and May 1917) under a byline by Wood. In Wood's *New York Times* obituary, "Beatrice Wood, 105, Potter and Mama of Dada, Is

Dead," May 14, 1998, A-15, this notation appears: "Wood defended
Duchamp's infamous urinal, rejected by the jury of the 1917 Indepen-
dents exhibition, with a sentence usually attributed to Duchamp himself: 'The only works of art America has given are her plumbing and her
bridges.'" The statement probably has been wrongly attributed to
Duchamp because Wood was writing about and defending his R. Mutt
urinal as art in her article.

27. John Kyle, "A Tribute to Othmar H. Ammann," *Port Authority Review*
4, no. 1 (1966), 3–8.

28. Quoted in Petroski, *Engineers of Dreams*, 317.

29. Bulletin 25 of the IABSE, reprint of a paper read in New York in September 1968. Stüssi was head of the Engineering Department of
Ammann's alma mater, the Polytechnic Institute in Zurich.

30. Ammann, "The Hell Gate Arch Bridge," 863.

31. On the occasion of the dedication of Ammann College at Stony Brook
University, February 18, 1968. Quoted in Leon Katz, "A Poet in Steel,"
Portfolio 1, no. 2 (Summer 1988), 36.

Chapter 6. "The Martha" and the Bus Station

1. E-mails from Bob Durando, June 29 and 30, 2006.

2. Margot Ammann Durrer, interview, January 26, 2007.

3. Port Authority press releases, August 29, 1962. For the water show, see
Joseph C. Ingraham, "Lower Deck of George Washington Bridge Is
Opened," *New York Times*, August 30, 1962, 1.

4. In 2004, *New York* magazine conducted a competition for fanciful
designs for a new bridge across the Hudson, with architect Richard
Meier as judge. See January 3, 2005, 14, 15.

5. Normally, the Defense Department requires two hundred feet of clearance for bridges.

6. Quoted in Edward Cohen et al., "The Engineer and His Works: A
Tribute to Othmar Hermann Ammann," *Annals of the New York
Academy of Sciences* 136, no. 23 (1966), 729.

7. Robert Carney, "The G.W.B.'s Believe-It-or-Not," *Bergen Record*,
October 18, 1981, A-3.

8. Othmar Ammann, "General Conception and Development of Design,"
George Washington Bridge Across the Hudson River at New York, N.Y.
(New York: American Society of Civil Engineers in Collaboration with
the Port of New York Authority), *Transactions of the A.S.C.E.* 97, no.
1818 (1933), 2.

9. Vicky Kelly, interview, May 24, 2006. The other major divisions of the Port Authority currently are Airports, Commerce (the port itself), and Rails (including the PATH train under the Hudson from New Jersey).

10. David Billington, *The Art of Structural Design: A Swiss Legacy* (Princeton: Princeton University Art Museum, 2003), 104.

11. Robert Caro, *The Power Broker: Robert Moses and the Fall of New York* (New York: Knopf, 1974), 898.

12. Philip Lopate, *Waterfront: A Journey Around Manhattan* (New York: Crown Publishers, 2004), 181.

13. However, the Upper Level of the Verrazano becomes a temporary "pedestrian" thoroughfare once a year when it serves as the starting point for the thirty thousand participants in the New York Marathon.

14. Paul Goldberger, *The City Observed, New York: A Guide to the Architecture of Manhattan* (New York: Random House, 1979), 327.

15. Ken Philmus, interview, June 14, 2006.

16. James Morris, *The Great Port: A Passage Through New York* (New York: Harcourt Brace, 1969), 157. Goldberger, *City Observed*, 327.

17. Ada Louise Huxtable, *Wall Street Journal*, online edition (www.opinion-journal.com), June 15, 2004.

18. A second casting of this bust may be found at Ammann's alma mater, the Swiss Polytechnic Institute in Zurich, Switzerland.

Chapter 7. Dramas, Dangers, and Disasters

1. Tom Toolen, "Did You Hear the One About the Chicken," *Bergen Record*, October 18, 1981, A-5.

2. Dierdre Carmody, "A 50-Year View of the George Washington Bridge," *New York Times*, October 10, 1981, Metro Section, 2.

3. Sydney Schanberg, "Plane Lands on George Washington Bridge," *New York Times*, December 27, 1965, 1. Also see Edward Hudson, "Pilot, 19, Defends Bridge Landing," *New York Times*, December 28, 1965, 29. A photograph of the crashed plane on the bridge appeared in *Life* magazine, January 7, 1966.

4. Rudy Larini, "Flight Crew Error Cited in Teterboro Crash," *Star-Ledger*, November 1, 2006, 13, 17.

5. Michael Teel, interviews, October 6 and December 7, 2005.

6. Steve Napolitano, interview, May 24, 2006.

7. Bruce Smith, "Charleston Native Who Received Heart on 9–11 Returns Home," Associated Press Newswires, October 31, 2002.

8. Jeffrey Page, "Bridge's Lower Level Needs a Higher Level of Security," *Record,* November 9, 2001, A-3. Bob Durando, interview, March 21, 2006. Steve Napolitano, interview, May 24, 2006.

9. Steve Napolitano, interview, May 24, 2006; Ken Philmus, interview, June 14, 2006.

10. Steve Napolitano, interview, May 24, 2006; Jerry Del Tufo, interview, April 17, 2006.

11. See Tad Friend, "Letter from California: Jumpers," *New Yorker,* October 13, 2003, 48.

12. *The Bridge,* 2006, produced and directed by Eric Steel. See Dennis Lim, "Mondo Multiplex: The Snuff Film Turns Respectable," *New York Times,* Arts and Leisure Section, October 22, 2006, 19.

13. See Friend, "Letter from California: Jumpers," 48.

14. In some models of the T-shirt the word "strong" has been substituted for "tough."

15. Sewell Chan, "Study Examines 'Suicide Tourism' in New York City," *New York Times,* City Room Blog, November 1, 2007, http://cityroom.blogs.nytimes.com/2007 11/01/study-examines-suicide.

16. Jon Robertson, interview, December 12, 2006.

17. Robert Carney, "The G.W.B.'s Believe-It-or-Not," *Bergen Record,* October 18, 1981, A-3.

18. Ken Philmus, interview, June 14, 2006.

19. Joanne Schneider, *Go Ahead, Jump! The Life Story of Billy Schneider* (New York: G.F.M. Publishers, 1998).

20. Bruce Weber, "Now a Caller from the G.W. Bridge: Stern to the Rescue," *New York Times,* December 8, 1994, 3.

Chapter 8. The George Washington Bridge in Literature

1. A somewhat different version of this anecdote appears in Nami Mun's story "On the Bus," *Iowa Review* 34, no. 2 (Fall 2004).

2. Edgar Rosenberg, "Hitler over My Head," *Judaism* (Summer 1999).

3. James Baldwin, *Another Country* (New York: Dell Publishers, 1962), 77, 78.

4. Howard Fast, *Redemption* (New York: Harcourt Brace, 1999), 8, 9, 15.

5. Anne Richardson Roiphe, *Up the Sandbox* (New York: Fawcett Crest, 1970), 30, 36, 38, 39.

6. Screenplay by Paul Zindel, directed by Irvin Kirshner, First Artists, 1972.

7. Nancy Herkness, *A Bridge to Love* (New York: Berkley Books, 2003), 59, 92, 93, 150, 158, 271, 278, 285, 294.

8. Alice Hoffman, *Property Of* (New York: Farrar, Straus & Giroux, 1977), chapter 2, 37–47. See *Looking for America on the New Jersey Turnpike*, by Angus Kress Gillespie and Michael Aaron Rockland (New Brunswick: Rutgers University Press, 1989), 147–149.

9. Richard Stark [Donald Westlake], *The Hunter* (New York: Allison & Bushby, 1962), 3. Issued in a later edition as *Point Blank*. The movie *Point Blank* was made by MGM, *Payback* by Icon Entertainment International.

10. Adrian McKinty, *Dead I Well May Be* (New York: Scribners, 2003), 193, 240, 241, 244, 250–256.

11. Philip Seplow, "Andy and the Tomato," from *Overgrown: Tales to Let You Know There Are Others in This World with Problems Worse than Yours* (Lincoln, NE: Writers Showcase, 2000), 75–107.

12. David Steinman, *Bridges and Their Builders* (New York: G. P. Putnam's Sons, 1941), v.

13. From the pamphlet *George Washington Bridge over the Hudson River Between New York and New Jersey, Addresses Delivered at Dedication, October 24, 1931*, published by the Port of New York Authority, 33, 34. I have abbreviated the poem; it does rather go on. The somewhat erratic punctuation is as published.

14. William Meredith, "The Cemetery Bridge," from *Poems Are Hard to Read* (Ann Arbor: University of Michigan Press, 1990), 55, 56.

15. Alicia Ostriker, " 'What Are Patterns For?' Anger and Polarization in Women's Poetry," *Feminist Studies* 10, no. 3 (Fall 1984), 492.

16. Alicia Ostriker, "The Bridge," from *The Crack in Everything* (Pittsburgh: University of Pittsburgh Press, 1990), 85.

17. Julius Henry Cohen, *They Builded Better than They Knew* (New York: Julian Messner, 1946), 123. Newman occasionally published poems in the *New York Times* and *Herald Tribune,* and a collection of his poetry was published after his death in 1954, edited by Jessie Wheeler Freeman and titled *Interior of a Question Mark: Poems by Israel Newman* (1957), but the G.W.B. poem isn't in it.

18. Joan Anderson, *Harry's Helicopter* (New York: Morrow Junior Books, 1990).

19. Maira Kalman, *Fireboat: The Heroic Adventures of the John J. Harvey* (New York: G. P. Putnam's Sons, 2002).

20. Buzz Aldrin, *Reaching for the Moon* (New York: Harper Collins Children's Books, 2005).

21. Manus Pinkwater, *Wingman* (New York: Dell Yearling Books, 1975).

22. Faith Ringgold, *Tar Beach* (New York: Crown Publishers, 1991). Faith Ringgold, interview, February 10, 2006. "A Literary Map of Manhattan," created by Randy Cohen, *New York Times Book Review*, June 2005, 1

23. *We Flew over the Bridge* (Boston: Little, Brown, 1995); *Aunt Harriet's Underground Railroad in the Sky* (New York: Crown, 1992). Faith Ringgold, interview, February 10, 2006.

24. Faith Ringgold, interview, February 10, 2006. One of Ringgold's works, "Sonny's Quilt," was inspired by the great jazzman Sonny Rollins, a childhood friend, known for going up on bridges and just blowing his horn.

25. Hildegarde Swift, *The Little Red Lighthouse and the Great Gray Bridge* (New York: Harcourt, 1942). *The Little Red Lighthouse and the Great Gray Bridge*, produced by Morton Schindel, Weston Woods Studios, n.d.

26. Dr. Ruth Westheimer, interview, September 16, 2006.

Chapter 9. The George Washington Bridge in the Other Arts

1. Gay Talese in the film "Bridging New York," part of the P.B.S. *Great Projects: The Building of America* series, written and produced by Daniel A. Miller, 2002.

2. A word of caution to anyone who finds yourself in my position: trying to discover all the films in which a certain bridge is part of the story. You will follow many false leads. A host of published sources, as well as the Internet, will mention scenes where the G.W.B. supposedly figures in the action, and they will be wrong. Well-meaning friends or relatives will also "help" by steering you to films in which any bridge but the George will be featured. I have watched movies to the point of bleary-eyed distraction waiting for a bridge to appear, and at last one or more has indeed made an appearance—and it was the Brooklyn or the Verrazano or the Golden Gate or the Queensboro or a bridge wholly unrecognizable to me.

3. *Network* (MGM, 1976) was directed by Sidney Lumet from a screenplay by Paddy Chayevsky. Both of them won Oscars.

4. *Force of Evil* (MGM, 1948) was based on the novel *Tucker's People*, by Ira Wolfert, who shares screenplay credit with director Abraham Polonsky.

5. *In The Cut* (Screen Gems, 2003) was directed by Jane Campion and based on the Susanna Moore novel by the same name.

6. *Ball of Fire* (Samuel Goldwyn, 1941) was directed by Howard Hawks and based on a story by Billy Wilder and Thomas Monroe.

7. *How to Marry a Millionaire,* directed by Jean Negulesco, Twentieth Century Fox, 1953.

8. *Desperately Seeking Susan,* directed by Susan Seidelman, Orion Pictures, 1985.

9. *Cop Land,* directed by James Mangold, Miramax, 1997.

10. *480 East 50th,* by Trista Conger, 1991.

11. *Land of Dreams,* by David Chapler, 1998.

12. *In the Heights,* Lin-Manuel Miranda, conceiver, composer, lyricist, and star.

13. *I Love Lucy,* episode 110 (season 4, episode 12), first aired January 10, 1955. This show apparently spawned a special edition of the board game Monopoly called "California, Here We Come."

14. The haiku was composed by Maurice Peterson in 1995; the video, including the haiku and Coltrane's music, was produced in 1998. It can be accessed via two sources: http://www.youtube.com/watch?v=ZQX-UhsbIX8; http://mauricepeterson.com/gwb. The quotation is from an e-mail from Maurice Peterson, November 30, 2007.

15. Letter from Valeri Larko, October 12, 2007.

16. E-mail from Dave Frieder, October 14, 2007.

17. Letter from Steven Siegel, October 7, 2007.

18. William Schuman, "George Washington Bridge," American Concert Band Masterpieces, Mercury Recording, Eastman Wind Ensemble, Frederick Fennell, conductor, 1958.

19. William Schuman, *Bergen Record,* October 18, 1981 (Fiftieth Anniversary Issue), A-2.

Chapter 10. Life Along the Walkways

1. Ron Marisco, "Higher Toll in Works for Hudson Crossings," *Star-Ledger,* October 31, 2007, 1, 5.

2. "Jersey Bridge Tolls End for Pedestrians," *New York Times,* May 29, 1940, 19.

3. See Jim Dwyer, "City Police Spied Broadly Before G.O.P. Convention," *New York Times,* March 25, 2007, 1, 34. Also see the *New York Times* lead editorial titled "The Police and the Spy Unit," March 27, 2007, A-18.

4. E-mail from Bob Durando, February 23, 2007.

5. Ralph Casey, interview on the north walkway, September 16, 2006.

6. Manhattan resident Robert Cavillieri, interview on the north walkway, October 24, 2006.

7. Eric Hollander, interview in Englewood Cliffs on June 7, 2006.

8. My interview with Denis Finnin began on the north walkway on June 21, 2006, and continued via e-mail on July 12, 2006.

9. See Michael Aaron Rockland, "Zen and the Art of Biking Route 1," *Snowshoeing Through Sewers* (New Brunswick: Rutgers University Press, 1994), 61–77.

10. Pearl Perkins, telephone interview, June 9, 2006.

11. Renee Piazza, interview, April 3, 2007. Renee made this trip with her father in 2000. Further information was garnered from Barbara Evans of the New York Chapter of the National Multiple Sclerosis Society via her e-mail to me of April 5, 2007.

12. Jeff Nordstedt, interview November 20, 2006.

13. Ray Muñoz, interview on the north walkway, September 20, 2006.

Chapter 11. The G.W.B. and Me

1. On 9/11 Fields was chief of security at the Port Authority Bus Terminal on Forty-first Street in Manhattan. Commandeering a bus, he and his men rushed down to the Twin Towers. The actor Jude Ciccolella plays Fields in Oliver Stone's film *World Trade Center*. Fields himself appears with debris falling all around him in the lobby of the North Tower of the World Trade Center in the horrifying 2002 documentary *9/11*, made by the French filmmakers Jules and Gedeon Naudet.

Selected Bibliography

Books and Articles

Ammann, Othmar. "Brobdingnagian Bridges." *Technology Review* 33, no. 9 (July 1931).

———. "The Cables of the Hudson River Bridge." New York: Port Authority, September 1930.

———. "The Hell Gate Arch Bridge and Approaches of the New York Connecting Railroad over the East River in New York City." *Transactions of the American Society of Civil Engineers* 82 (December 1918).

———. "Tentative Report on the Hudson River Bridge." In *Engineers as Writers*, ed. Walter J. Miller and Leo E. A. Saidla. New York, 1953.

Amman, Othmar, et al. *George Washington Bridge Across the Hudson River at New York, N.Y.* Vol. 97 of the *Transactions of the American Society of Civil Engineers*, nos. 1818–1825. New York: A.S.C.E./ Port of New York Authority, 1933.

Billington, David P. *The Art of Structural Design: A Swiss Legacy.* New Haven: Princeton University Art Museum in Association with Yale University Press, 2003.

———. *The Tower and the Bridge: The New Art of Structural Engineering.* New York: Basic Books, 1983.

Billington, David P., and Billington, David P., Jr. Chapter 8, "Ammann and the George Washington Bridge." In *Power, Speed, and Form: Engineers and the Making of the Twentieth Century.* Princeton: Princeton University Press, 2006.

Brown, David J., *Three Thousand Years of Defying Nature.* Buffalo: Firefly Books, 2005.

Caro, Robert. *The Power Broker: Robert Moses and the Fall of New York.* New York: Knopf, 1974.

Cohen, Edward. *The Legacy of Othmar H. Ammann.* New York: Ammann & Whitney, 1987.

Cohen, Edward, et al. "The Engineer and His Works: A Tribute to Othmar Hermann Ammann." *Annals of the New York Academy of Science* 136, no. 23 (1966).

Doig, Jameson W. *Empire on the Hudson: Entrepreneurial Vision and Political Power at the Port of New York Authority.* New York: Columbia University Press, 2001.

———. "Politics and the Engineering Mind: O. H. Ammann and the Hidden Story of the George Washington Bridge." In *Building the Public City,* ed. David Perry. Thousand Oaks, CA: Sage Publications, 1995. Also published in *Yearbook of German-American Studies* 25 (1990).

Durrer, Margot Amman. "Memories of My Father." *Swiss American Historical Review,* April 4, 1979.

Geis, Joseph. *Bridges and Men.* Garden City, N.Y.: Doubleday, 1963.

Goldberger, Paul. *The City Observed, New York: A Guide to the Architecture of Manhattan.* New York: Random House, 1979.

Hertzberg, Hendrik. "Gorgeous George." *New Yorker* 77, no. 5 (March 26, 2001).

Jablow, Valerie. "Othmar Ammann's Glory." *Smithsonian* 30, no. 7 (October 1999).

Katz, Leon. "A Poet in Steel." *Portfolio* (published by the Port Authority) 1, no. 2 (Summer 1988).

Kouwenhoven, John. Chapter 10, "Stone, Steel and Jazz." In *The Arts in Modern American Civilization.* New York: W. W. Norton, 1948.

Kyle, John M. "A Tribute to Othmar H. Ammann." *Port Authority Review* 4, no. 1 (1966).

Macaulay, David. *Building Big.* Boston: Houghton Mifflin, 2000.

Morris, James. *The Great Port: A Passage Through New York.* New York: Harcourt Brace, 1969.

Petroski, Henry. *Engineers of Dreams: Great Bridge Builders and the Spanning of America.* New York: Knopf, 1995.

———. Chapter 13, "The Ups and Downs of Bridges." In *To Engineer Is Human: The Role of Failure in Successful Design.* New York: Vintage Books, 1992.

Quinn, Peter. "Bridge Builder." *American Heritage* 53, no. 5 (October 2002).

Rastorfer, Darl. "George Washington Bridge: A Timeless Marvel." Port Authority of New York and New Jersey: Darl Rastorfer and Associates, 2006.

———. *Six Bridges: The Legacy of Othmar H. Ammann.* New Haven: Yale University Press, 2000.

Reier, Sharon. *The Bridges of New York.* New York: Quadrant Press, 1977.

Richman, Steven. *The Bridges of New Jersey: Portrait of Garden State Crossings.* New Brunswick: Rutgers University Press, 2005.

Steinman, David B., and Sara Ruth Watson. Chapter 16, "Great Suspension Bridges." In *Bridges and Their Builders.* New York: G. P. Putnam, 1941.

Stüssi, F. "From Leonardo Da Vinci to Othmar H. Ammann." Paper read at the Eighth Congress of the International Association for Bridge and Structural Engineering, September 1968, published in I.A.B.S.E. Bulletin 25.

Tobin, James. Chapter 6, "Ammann's Bridge." In *Great Projects: The Epic Story of the Building of America From the Taming of the Mississippi to the Invention of the Internet.* New York: The Free Press, 2001.

Woolf, S. J. "A Master Builder Looks Ahead." *New York Times Magazine,* April 15, 1934.

Wisehart, M. K. "The Greatest Bridge in the World and the Man Who Is Building It." *American Magazine,* no. 34 (June 1928).

Documentary Films

"Bridging New York." Part of the P.B.S. *Great Projects: The Building of America series.* Written and produced by Daniel A. Miller, 2002.

Building the Bridge (a silent black-and-white film; unedited footage). Port Authority of New York and New Jersey, 1931.

George Washington Bridge: Crossing the Hudson. Directed by Mark Daniels, 2002.

Handbike Movie. Written and directed by Martin Bruch, Satel Films, 2003.

Modern Marvels: The George Washington Bridge. Written and produced by Henry Schipper, 2004.

Index

About the Author

MICHAEL AARON ROCKLAND is a professor of American Studies at Rutgers University. His early career was in the U.S. diplomatic service. He is the author of ten previous books, three of which have received special notice. His first book, *Sarmiento's Travels in the United States in 1847*, was chosen by *Washington Post Book World* as one of the fifty best books of the year. His novel, *A Bliss Case*, was a *New York Times* Notable Book of the Year. And a book he co-wrote, *Looking for America on the New Jersey Turnpike* (Rutgers University Press), was chosen by the New Jersey State Library as one of the "Ten Best Books Ever Written about New Jersey or by a New Jerseyan." Rockland is a contributing editor at *New Jersey Monthly* and has worked in both film and television production.